THE FIRST DAY AT GETTYSBURG, JULY 1, 1863

CASEMATE | ILLUSTRATED

THE FIRST DAY AT GETTYSBURG, JULY 1, 1863

James A. Hessler

CIS0049

Published in 2025 by
CASEMATE PUBLISHERS
1950 Lawrence Road, Havertown, PA 19083, USA
and
47 Church Street, Barnsley, S70 2AS, UK

Published in conjunction with Savas Beatie.

Paperback edition: ISBN 978-1-63624-479-2
Digital edition: ISBN 978-1-63624-480-8

A CIP record for this book is available from the British Library.

Maps by Battlefield Design
Design by Myriam Bell
Printed and bound in the United Kingdom by Short Run Press

For a complete list of Casemate titles, please contact:

CASEMATE PUBLISHERS (US)
Telephone (610) 853-9131
Fax (610) 853-9146
Email: casemate@casematepublishers.com
www.casematepublishers.com

CASEMATE PUBLISHERS (UK)
Telephone (0)1226 734350
Email: casemate@casemateuk.com
www.casemateuk.com

Half-title image: Major General John Reynolds. (Library of Congress)
Title-page image: Modern view from the Lutheran Seminary cupola looking west toward McPherson Ridge. (Rob Williams, Seminary Ridge Museum and Education Center)

Acknowledgements
Our objective was to create a concise narrative of the July 1 battle at Gettysburg supplemented by photography and maps. I want to thank my friends and colleagues who assisted in achieving that task. You made this a much better book. First, thanks to Ted Savas (publisher of my three previous books) who requested that I tackle this project. Thanks also to the team at Casemate Publishers for putting it together. Fellow Gettysburg Licensed Battlefield Guides Susan Stromello and John Zervas peer-reviewed the manuscript and offered useful feedback. Thanks also to my friends and colleagues Wayne Motts, Eric Lindblade, and Dave Powell for reading early proof versions. For the images, my thanks to talented friends Phil Spaugy, Lynn Heller, Rob Williams and Codie Eash (Seminary Ridge Museum and Education Center), Tracy Baer, Robert Housch (Gettysburg Daily.com), and Jody Wilson for taking some of the modern photographs used throughout this book. Thank you to Jim Schmick (Civil War and More), Gary Kross, and Lance Herdegen for generously providing historic images from their personal collections. My appreciation also to John Hoptak (Gettysburg National Military Park), Jack Owens (Shenandoah Valley Battlefields National Historic District), and Mary Laura Kludy (VMI Archives) for assisting with access to images in their collections. Last but certainly not least, thanks to my wife Michele for her patience and support while I grudgingly authored another book during a period of major upheaval in our lives. Thank you for tolerating all of it … again!

Contents

Timeline

1863
April 30–May 6
General Robert E. Lee's Army of Northern Virginia defeats the Army of the Potomac under Major General Joseph Hooker at the battle of Chancellorsville.

May 11–15
General Lee meets Confederate political leaders in Richmond for a multi-day conference to discuss strategic plans. Lee obtains permission to initiate a summer campaign in Pennsylvania.

June 3
Lee's Army of Northern Virginia begins moving northward after withdrawing from Fredericksburg, Virginia.

June 9
Cavalry and infantry clash at the large battle of Brandy Station.

June 10
Hooker's Army of the Potomac in pursuit of Lee's army.

June 13–15
Confederate Lieutenant General Richard Ewell's Second Corps moves north through the Shenandoah Valley and defeats Union garrison at second battle of Winchester.

June 15
Brigadier General Albert Jenkins's cavalry brigade becomes the first of the Confederate forces to enter Pennsylvania.

June 17–21
Union cavalry attempts to push through Confederate cavalry screens and locate Lee's army, leading to cavalry actions at Aldie, Middleburg, and Upperville in the Loudon Valley.

June 19
The leading Confederate infantry in Ewell's Second Corps has crossed the Potomac River into Maryland.

June 25
Major General J. E. B. Stuart and three brigades of cavalry depart from Lee's army. Stuart is expected to gather supplies, do damage, and reconnect with the main body of Lee's army. Stuart loses contact for one week, leaving Lee unaware of enemy movements.

June 26	Confederate forces under Major General Jubal Early briefly enter Gettysburg. Early's men spare the town and depart after attempting to requisition supplies from town leaders.
June 27	General Hooker offers his resignation as commander of the Army of the Potomac.
June 28	Major General George Meade replaces Hooker as commander of the Army of the Potomac. General Lee receives intelligence from a spy that the Union army is advancing into Pennsylvania. Lee issues orders to concentrate his army east of South Mountain.
June 30	Brigadier General John Buford's Union cavalry and Confederate infantry under Brigadier General Johnston Pettigrew nearly collide at Gettysburg. Pettigrew reports the encounter to his superiors who decide to move toward Gettysburg in greater force on July 1. Union Major General John Reynolds also receives orders to march his First Corps toward Gettysburg on July 1 with Major General Oliver Howard's Eleventh Corps in close support.
July 1	First day of the battle of Gettysburg.

▲ Monuments to Union generals John Buford (foreground) and John Reynolds along the Chambersburg Pike west of Gettysburg. (Photo by Lynn Heller)

Introduction

The American Civil War entered its third summer in 1863. In the war's Eastern Theater, the Army of the Potomac struggled to gain battlefield victories for the North, while President Abraham Lincoln searched for a reliable general to lead the army. In the South, although Confederate General Robert E. Lee scored several military triumphs, the war effort faced several challenges.

"What will the country say? Oh, what will the country say?" President Abraham Lincoln uttered that question after another defeat by the Army of the Potomac at the battle of Chancellorsville. Fought during early May 1863, this was the second massive defeat suffered by Lincoln's primary Eastern Theater army during the past six months.

That same army previously suffered more than 12,600 total casualties against General Robert E. Lee's Army of Northern Virginia at the battle of Fredericksburg, Virginia, in December 1862. Under the command of Major General Ambrose Burnside at Fredericksburg, Union generals obligingly threw attack after attack against the Confederates' prepared defensive positions with predictable results. Fredericksburg was a humiliating and costly defeat for Burnside's army. After poor January weather derailed Burnside's attempt to outmaneuver Lee's army in what became known derisively as the Mud March, these failures forced Lincoln to replace Burnside as army commander with Major General Joseph Hooker.

Joseph "Fighting Joe" Hooker, nicknamed due to an erroneous press report, was a West Point graduate who performed commendably at lower levels and rose through the army. Yet, Lincoln had reservations about promoting Hooker. Joe Hooker was known personally as a drinker and womanizer, neither of which was uncommon in the United States Army. The president believed correctly that this confident and ambitious general mixed politics too freely with his profession. (A characteristic that was also too common in the Army of the Potomac's upper

◀ Major General Joseph Hooker received command of the Army of the Potomac in January 1863. President Lincoln held reservations about promoting Hooker, due to Fighting Joe's previous statement that the government needed a dictator. (Library of Congress)

echelons.) "I have heard," the desperate Lincoln told Hooker, "in such way as to believe it, of your recently saying that both the Army and the Government needed a Dictator. ... Only those generals who gain successes can set up dictators. What I now ask of you is military success, and I will risk the dictatorship."

Hooker's military strategy started with great promise but ended badly. In April, he developed a bold plan of maneuver to strike Lee's army opposite Fredericksburg. While a portion of his army remained near Fredericksburg to keep Lee's attention occupied there, the majority of Hooker's infantry marched upriver and crossed the Rappahannock and Rapidan rivers to concentrate in Lee's rear near the crossroads residence of Chancellorsville. By April 30, Hooker's initial movements appeared to work perfectly. "May God have mercy on General Lee," the boastful Hooker wrote in a self-congratulatory order, "for I will have none."

Unfortunately for Hooker, once Lee learned of these moves, he quickly divided his army and sent Lieutenant General Thomas J. "Stonewall" Jackson westward

▶ General Robert E. Lee led the Army of Northern Virginia from June 1862. His victories against Northern generals frustrated the Lincoln administration and renewed confidence within the Confederacy. Lee convinced the Confederate government to bring the war into Pennsylvania during the summer of 1863. (Library of Congress)

from Fredericksburg to confront Hooker near Chancellorsville. Surprised by Lee's aggression, Hooker suddenly lost his nerve and the initiative. Fighting Joe abandoned his offensive strategy as he fell back into a defensive posture around Chancellorsville. From May 1–3, Lee and Jackson boldly divided their inferior numbers to strike with maximum effect, outmaneuvered, and outfought an increasingly befuddled Hooker. By May 6, a humiliated and thoroughly beaten Army of the Potomac retreated across the Rappahannock River.

Hooker had committed roughly 100,000 men and been beaten by almost half that number under General Lee. The battle was the bloodiest in American history up to that time with more than 30,000 combined losses. More than 17,000 of those casualties were in the Army of the Potomac. Lincoln had another battlefield disaster on his hands.

The Fredericksburg and Chancellorsville defeats offered applicable lessons for Gettysburg later that summer. Lee's Fredericksburg victory demonstrated the value of defensive tactics if enemy troops were cooperative enough to make assaults across open fields against well-prepared positions. On the other hand, Chancellorsville demonstrated that Lee's perpetually outnumbered army could succeed with audacity, maneuver, and aggression. These outcomes raised morale in Lee's army while correspondingly lowering spirits among Hooker's men. Some of the Northern soldiers felt that they had been outgeneraled but not outfought, while Lee's men increasingly felt that their general could lead them to victory anywhere.

These defeats also brought out the worst characteristics in the Northern army. Hooker built a network of loyal cronies that included his chief of staff

Major General Daniel Butterfield and the politically appointed Major General Daniel Sickles who commanded the army's Third Corps. Several officers, such as Fifth Corps commander Major General George Meade, were excluded from this circle. After Chancellorsville, Hooker and Meade engaged in a squabble over whether Meade was among those generals who counseled for a Union withdrawal after Chancellorsville. (Meade did not support such a move.) Some generals began grumbling that they would no longer serve under Hooker. The Northern newspapers speculated on a replacement.

The need to find scapegoats zeroed in on the heavily German immigrant population of the Eleventh Corps under Major General Oliver Howard. On May 2 at Chancellorsville, Stonewall Jackson's powerful flank attack hit Howard's unprepared position and many Eleventh Corps soldiers fled in shock and surprise. Whether deserved or not, feelings in the army ran hard against Howard's "Flying Dutchman" as a key cause of the Chancellorsville defeat.

As the summer of 1863 approached, the Army of the Potomac was reeling once again from their latest battlefield defeat. Confidence was high within Robert E. Lee's Army of Northern Virginia, but the Confederate war effort faced their own organizational issues and strategic problems.

▲ The battle of Fredericksburg in December 1862 was a one-sided victory by Lee's army over the Army of the Potomac. This Alfred Waud sketch illustrates one of the Northern army's several repeated assaults made against the Southerners' defensive positions at Marye's Heights. (Library of Congress)

◄ Chancellorsville was another Confederate victory, as Robert E. Lee repeatedly divided his outnumbered army against an increasingly befuddled General Hooker. Hooker's headquarters at the Chancellor house sat in ruins afterwards. (Francis Miller, ed., *The Photographic History of the Civil War in Ten Volumes* [New York, 1911], 2:126)

Lee and Hooker's Campaign Begins

Both armies planned and reorganized for the summer campaign following Chancellorsville. General Lee promoted two new corps commanders to replace Stonewall Jackson and authorized a risky assignment for cavalry commander J. E. B. Stuart. In the Army of the Potomac, General Hooker was unable to ascertain Lee's intentions as the Army of Northern Virginia began their move northward.

The massive casualties of Chancellorsville required reorganization in both armies. In the Army of the Potomac, Major General Darius Couch was the army's senior corps commander but requested reassignment rather than continue under Hooker. As a result, Major General Winfield S. Hancock received command of Couch's Second Corps. The army lost the experienced Couch but elevated the aggressive Hancock. Even more importantly, the army's strength fell by about 20% during spring 1863 as approximately 23,000 men departed upon the expiration of some two-year and nine-month volunteer enlistments.

Despite being the victor at Fredericksburg and Chancellorsville, Robert E. Lee's smaller Army of Northern Virginia suffered more than 18,000 hard-to-replace casualties in the two battles combined. Although Lee's army had humiliated their opponents militarily, strategically Lee gained no ground. By late spring 1863 the two sides were basically where they had started the year: locked in a stalemate along the Rappahannock River at Fredericksburg.

Confederate Second Corps commander Stonewall Jackson was the most significant of Lee's losses. Jackson's own men shot him accidentally in the darkness on May 2, and he succumbed to complications on May 10. Lee acted upon a prior notion that three smaller corps might be easier to manage than two large ones. He assigned Jackson's corps to recently promoted Lieutenant General Richard Ewell and created a Third Corps for newly promoted Lieutenant General Ambrose Powell (or "A. P.") Hill. Both Ewell and Hill had demonstrated their ability to lead a division, but neither man had experience at corps command. At every level of Lee's army, other officers advanced up the chain of command to fill vacancies, while some who were bypassed questioned whether there was too much "Virginia bias" in the promotions. Lee also counted on his veteran soldiers, who were more confident than ever following the recent victories.

▲◀ Lieutenant General Richard Ewell earned promotion to command the Second Corps in Lee's army prior to Gettysburg. The eccentric Ewell performed capably at lower levels and during the early phases of the Gettysburg campaign, but his ability to take the initiative would be called into question late on July 1. (Library of Congress)

▲ Lieutenant General A. P. Hill received the new Third Corps in Lee's army. His famed "Light Division" performed admirably in earlier engagements, but he reportedly suffered from ill health on July 1 as his corps opened the battle at Gettysburg. (Library of Congress)

◀ Lieutenant General James Longstreet retained command of the First Corps. Longstreet's corps were not a factor on July 1 at Gettysburg, but his belief that Lee agreed to fight a defensive battle planted seeds of controversy in the Gettysburg historiography. (Library of Congress)

The Army of Northern Virginia's First Corps remained under Lieutenant General James Longstreet. Lee's "Old War Horse" and senior subordinate performed admirably at Fredericksburg behind prepared defensive positions. Longstreet missed Chancellorsville's offensive successes, however, due to being on an independent assignment gathering desperately needed supplies around Suffolk, Virginia. Longstreet returned to Lee's army prior to the Gettysburg campaign.

Lee's Lieutenants

Due to the death of General Thomas "Stonewall" Jackson, two of Robert E. Lee's three corps commanders were new to their roles during the Gettysburg campaign. Both men were skilled officers, yet historians debate whether Lee should have exercised more direct oversight at Gettysburg due to their inexperience at the corps level.

Second Corps—Lieutenant General Richard Ewell

The 46-year-old new commander of the Second Corps was known as "Old Bald Head" or "Baldy" to his friends. An 1840 West Point graduate, Ewell had long service on the frontier and Mexican War before resigning his United States Army commission in May 1861. He was wounded in a skirmish at Fairfax Court House on May 31, giving him the distinction of being the first field-grade officer wounded in the Civil War.

Ewell received a commission as a brigadier general in June 1861 and promotion to major general in January 1862. Ewell served alongside Jackson through the famed Valley campaign in Virginia and other battles of 1862. At the battle of Groveton in August 1862, Ewell received a severe wound in the leg which required an amputation. Ewell's promotion to lieutenant general after Chancellorsville was dated one day earlier than A. P. Hill's, making Old Bald Head the third-highest ranking general in the Army of Northern Virginia, behind only Lee and Longstreet.

Ewell had an eccentric and profane personality. In late May 1863, he married his first cousin, Lizinka Campbell Brown. (He referred to his new bride as "Mrs. Brown.") A new romance and a new disability might have cooled some of Ewell's earlier aggressions. Ewell also seemed to require precise instructions, unlike his more flexible predecessor Jackson. Some historians question whether these factors hindered his Gettysburg performance, although he performed well during the early campaign.

Third Corps—Lieutenant General Ambrose Powell (A. P.) Hill

The commander of the newly created Third Corps graduated from the West Point class of 1847. Hill resigned from the United States Army in March 1861 and became colonel of the 13th Virginia Infantry. Hill received promotion to brigadier general in February 1862 and performed well during the Peninsula campaign. As a result, he received promotion to major general in May 1862. Hill fought in the Seven Days, Cedar Mountain, and Second Manassas. Hill became an important part of Stonewall Jackson's command, although the two generals did not get along, quarreled, and Hill sometimes found himself under arrest. (Hill also feuded with James Longstreet.) His division received the nickname the "Light Division" to convey a reputation for speed and agility. At Antietam, Hill might have saved Lee's army as the Light Division marched from Harpers Ferry and counterattacked against a threat to Lee's right flank.

A. P. Hill's Gettysburg performance is an enigma. His Third Corps was the first to engage on July 1 and remained active during all three days, yet evidence of Hill directly leading his corps is scarce. A sickly man, Hill caught gonorrhea during his West Point years, causing medical complications that plagued him for the rest of his life. Some accounts have Hill in his sickbed with illness on the morning of July 1, an unfortunate time to go down for a general who had such a solid record up to this point in the war.

Longstreet later insisted he and Lee agreed on fighting a defensive battle "in a position of our own choosing" as the "ruling idea" for the campaign. Fredericksburg had shown the "advantage of receiving instead of giving attack" and the need to minimize costly losses. Lee was unlikely to have entered into such an agreement with his subordinate beforehand, but later acknowledged in his own report, "It had not been intended to fight a general battle at such a distance from our base, unless attacked by the enemy." It appears likely that defensive tactics would supplement an offensive strategy if circumstances required.

Notwithstanding their recent victories, the Confederacy faced uncertainties. Food and supplies for Lee's army were running dangerously low in Virginia. In the Western Theater, General Ulysses S. Grant's presence near the vital city of Vicksburg threatened to cut off Confederate control of the Mississippi River. Confederate President Jefferson Davis and Secretary of War James Seddon considered transferring portions of Lee's army to that theater, but Lee opposed that move.

Earlier that winter, Jackson's topographical engineer Jedediah Hotchkiss received orders to prepare a map extending to Harrisburg, Pennsylvania, and on to Philadelphia. Chancellorsville and Jackson's death temporarily interrupted such plans. In mid-May, Lee met with Davis and Seddon in Richmond to discuss strategies. Lee favored a counteroffensive in the Eastern Theater to gather supplies in the North and disrupt Federal campaigns in the South for the summer. The Southerners designated the Pennsylvania state capital of Harrisburg as an objective at some point. Lee's threats to the heavily populated and resource-rich Pennsylvania would certainly disrupt any

of Joe Hooker's plans in Virginia, but such an incursion might even force Grant away from the Mississippi and relieve pressure in the West.

When Grant began his siege of Vicksburg, the Confederate high command agreed to Lee's proposed "transfer of the scene of hostilities north of the Potomac," despite reservations on President Davis's part. While some historians have characterized Lee's invasion as a supply raid, and there is no doubt that resupply was an important objective, Lee later emphasized that moving north "might offer a fair opportunity to strike a blow at the army then commanded by General Hooker." Lee's objectives were multi-faceted.

Lee began troop withdrawal from Fredericksburg on June 3. The Army of

▼ Major General James Ewell Brown Stuart capably commanded Lee's cavalry division. Stuart's absence from June 25 to July 2 deprived Lee of intelligence on enemy movements. Some literature has labeled Stuart's ride north as a vain attempt at gaining attention, but Lee gave Stuart some discretion in selecting his route. (Library of Congress)

▲ This Edwin Forbes drawing depicts some of the cavalry fighting at Brandy Station. Although infantry was also involved in the battle, the Union cavalry gained increased confidence during the opening stages of the Gettysburg campaign. (Library of Congress)

▼ Major General Alfred Pleasonton commanded the Cavalry Corps within the Army of the Potomac. Pleasonton's forces embarrassed J. E. B. Stuart at Brandy Station, although some criticized him for not scoring a decisive victory. Pleasonton led the cavalry during a critical period, but historians question his competency and overshadow him in favor of subordinates such as John Buford. (Library of Congress)

Northern Virginia's strength stood at roughly 72,000 men in three infantry corps, artillery, and cavalry. Hooker and his staff became aware of Lee's activities as early as June 4, but they remained unsure of their opponent's intent or destination. Lee's army headed primarily northwesterly toward the Shenandoah Valley, where the Blue Ridge Mountains would help screen their advance.

The first major engagement of the Gettysburg campaign occurred on June 9 at the battle of Brandy Station in Culpeper County, Virginia. Major General James Ewell Brown ("Jeb" or J. E. B) Stuart, the dashing commander of Lee's cavalry division, was bivouacked in the vicinity with approximately 9,500 men. General Hooker was aware of the Confederates' presence near Culpeper and ordered his own cavalry under Major General Alfred Pleasonton to "disperse and destroy" the enemy.

Pleasonton surprised Stuart early on the morning of June 9, when the Federals launched a two-pronged attack with about 11,000 cavalrymen and infantrymen. Pleasonton was forced to withdraw after day-long fighting, leaving Stuart in command of the field. Yet, some Southern newspapers were critical of Stuart being surprised. Brandy Station is considered the first time that Union cavalry matched their counterparts on the battlefield, although Northern infantry contributed too. By June 10, Hooker's army was in pursuit but still unsure of Lee's objectives.

The next major clash occurred near Winchester, Virginia. The second battle of Winchester occurred on June 13–15, 1863. (The first battle of Winchester was a Confederate victory by Jackson in 1862.) General Ewell's Second Corps led the Army of Northern Virginia's movement through the Shenandoah Valley with orders to clear the way of opposition. Major General Robert Milroy led Winchester's garrison of approximately 6,900 men. General Ewell and his division commanders knew the area well, so they split their forces into two flanking movements, surrounded, and overwhelmed Milroy's command. The Confederates captured roughly 4,000 Yankees along with artillery, horses, and large amounts of supplies. The Northern war machine was embarrassed yet again, and General Ewell acquitted himself well in his first action as a corps commander.

General Pleasonton's attempts to push through Stuart's screen in the mountain gaps and locate the remainder of Lee's army led to three cavalry actions at Aldie, Middleburg, and Upperville in the Loudon Valley between June 17–21. Although these actions were relatively small, both sides fought doggedly for control of the gaps. By the conclusion of the Upperville engagement, Stuart succeeded in preventing Pleasonton's cavalry from accurately assessing the location of Lee's infantry.

If J. E. B. Stuart's men performed well in these early actions, what occurred afterward has been long steeped in controversy. Stuart proposed to Lee and Longstreet that he ride eastward through a gap in the Bull Run Mountains, gain the enemy's rear, place himself between the Yankees and Washington, and create havoc before crossing into Maryland and rejoining the army north of the Potomac. Lee approved the plan and Longstreet also endorsed it.

Lee directed Stuart to leave two brigades behind to guard the Blue Ridge and observe Hooker's movements, but also gave Stuart discretion "to judge whether you can pass around their army without hindrance." Communications emphasized that Stuart was expected to do "all the damage you can" and "collect all the supplies you can use for the army" but once across the Potomac, Lee underscored Stuart "must move on" and take position on Ewell's right.

Stuart elected to take his three favorite brigades of slightly fewer than 5,000 men under Brigadier General Wade Hampton, Brigadier General Fitzhugh Lee, and Colonel John Chambliss on his assignment. While there was logic in taking the best brigades on a long and dangerous ride, Stuart left two brigades behind under less-favored brigadier generals Beverly Roberston and William "Grumble" Jones to observe Hooker. Stuart instructed

▼ When J. E. B. Stuart departed the army to begin his ride north, Brigadier General Beverly Robertson remained behind with his own brigade and William "Grumble" Jones's brigade to observe the Army of the Potomac's movements. Robertson was to report any important information on enemy movements and then rejoin the main army. (Library of Congress)

▲ Brigadier General Albert Jenkins's cavalry brigade, often referred to as mounted infantry, accompanied Ewell's Second Corps into Pennsylvania. Jenkins provided Ewell with screening, foraging, and scouting duties. Another brigade under Brigadier General John Imboden, which was formed of men who were more armed riders than trained cavalry, acted semi-independently for much of the campaign. Jenkins and Imboden provided Lee's army with some cavalry support in Stuart's absence. (Ezra J. Warner, *Generals in Gray: Lives of the Confederate Commanders* [Baton Rouge, LA: 2013], 154)

brigade, often referred to as mounted infantry, accompanied Ewell's corps into Pennsylvania. Jenkins provided Ewell with screening, foraging, and scouting duties. Another brigade under Brigadier General John Imboden, which was formed more of armed riders than trained cavalry, acted semi-independently for much of the campaign. Neither Jenkins nor Imboden were in position, however, to keep an eye on Hooker's army. That assignment was expected of Stuart's two brigades under Robertson and Jones.

On June 15, Jenkins's mounted infantry became the first of the Confederate forces to enter Pennsylvania. The lead infantry of Ewell's Second Corps began crossing the Potomac into Maryland on that same date. Ewell's men advanced deeper into Pennsylvania, while Hill's Third Corps and then Longstreet proceeded to cross the Potomac between June 24–26.

By June 27, part of Ewell and Jenkins's commands approached Carlisle and the Susquehanna River beyond. Jubal Early's division of that corps moved eastward toward York. Robert E. Lee crossed the Mason–Dixon line on that date as Hill and Longstreet concentrated near Chambersburg, Pennsylvania. Ewell's progress was such that the Second Corps risked being too far from support in the event of a conflict. All that was missing was Stuart and any reliable intelligence on his location or that of the enemy's.

In fact, neither side seemed to know what Hooker's army was doing. Pennsylvania was under enemy occupation and the Army of the Potomac was not there to defend the citizens of the critically important Keystone State. President Lincoln and General in Chief Henry Halleck continued to lose faith in Joe Hooker. Halleck and Hooker never liked each other anyways, dating

Robertson, the senior officer over Jones, to guard the mountain passes, observe the Union army, and rejoin Lee's infantry at the first sign of enemy movement.

Stuart and his three brigades departed the army at 1:00 a.m. on June 25. Stuart's plan went awry almost immediately, as infantry from Hancock's Second Corps inadvertently blocked the proposed route. Rather than retracing his movements, Stuart used his discretion to ride even farther east than expected and attempted to pass around the Federal army. Already off schedule, the stage was set to leave Lee "blind" for the next week as his "eyes and ears" under Stuart disappeared.

Stuart's departure did not leave Lee devoid of any cavalry. Brigadier General Albert Jenkins's cavalry

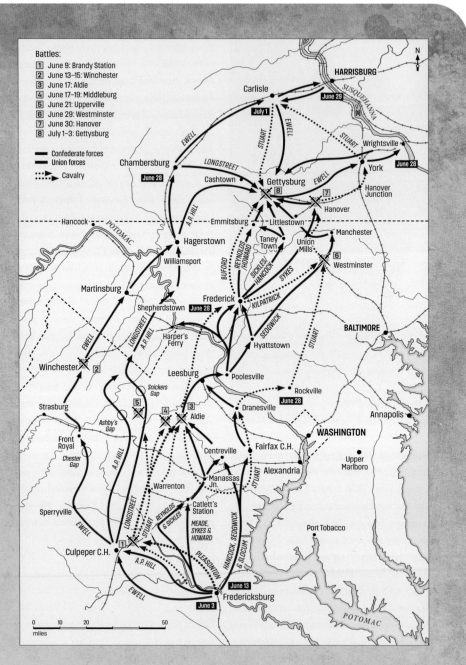

Battles:
1. June 9: Brandy Station
2. June 13–15: Winchester
3. June 17: Aldie
4. June 17–19: Middleburg
5. June 21: Upperville
6. June 29: Westminster
7. June 30: Hanover
8. July 1–3: Gettysburg

▬▬ Confederate forces
▬▬ Union forces
•••▶ Cavalry

▲ Movements of both armies from June 3–July 1.

Profile:
Major General George Meade (1815–72)

George Gordon Meade was 47 years old in the summer of 1863. The son of a prominent Philadelphia family, Meade was born in Cadiz, Spain, on December 31, 1815. His father was serving there as a U.S. naval agent, but the family suffered financial setbacks when Meade's father supported Spain during the Napoleonic Wars. Meade's family returned to America in 1817. A military education was not George's first choice, but due to the family's financial situation Meade entered the United State Military Academy at West Point. He graduated 19th in the class of 1835. Second Lieutenant Meade served briefly during the

Seminole War before resigning his commission to work as a civil engineer. He rejoined the army in 1842 in the Corps of Topographical Engineers. Meade subsequently served during the Mexican War and was present at several battles, although he saw no major combat. Captain Meade returned to topographical work after the Mexican War. He constructed lighthouses, improved harbors, and oversaw surveys.

With the onset of the Civil War, Meade received a commission as brigadier general of volunteers with the Pennsylvania Reserves in August 1861. Meade was wounded in action while leading his brigade at Glendale in late June 1862. He returned by the end of summer and led a division in the First Corps under Joe Hooker. Meade temporarily led the corps when Hooker suffered a wound at Antietam.

General John Reynolds, and not Meade, received command of the First Corps in late 1862 during another army reorganization. Meade and Reynolds were on friendly terms, but professional rivalry existed, and Meade expressed frustration at being passed over. Meade acknowledged privately that while he felt his own record merited consideration, Reynolds had stronger political connections and typically made a more favorable impression.

Serving under Reynolds, Meade's division fought well at Fredericksburg and exploited a gap in Stonewall Jackson's defensive line. Meade was repulsed, however, after receiving no support. Meade angrily blamed

◄ Major General George Gordon Meade received the unenviable promotion to command the Army of the Potomac on June 28, 1863. A modest yet sometimes short-tempered general, Meade had his supporters and detractors within the army, while many were skeptical of another command change. Meade quickly got his army moving north from Frederick, Maryland, and caught Lee by surprise at Gettysburg. (Library of Congress)

General David Birney of the Third Corps for lack of assistance, and this led to bad blood against Meade in the Third Corps. Yet, Meade wrote privately that Reynolds was also partially responsible for the mistake. "I think he [Reynolds] was in some measure responsible for my not being supported on the 13th as he was commanding the corps & had the authority to order up other troops —and it was his business to have seen that I was properly supported." Nevertheless, Meade and Reynolds continued cordial relations. Meade subsequently received command of the Fifth Corps and led it at Chancellorsville. This promotion created friction with the prior commander, General Dan Butterfield, who unfortunately served as Meade's chief of staff during the subsequent Gettysburg campaign.

George Meade was a devoted family person who corresponded frequently with his wife while in the field. He was known to be short-tempered with others, however, and earned the nickname "Old Snapping Turtle." Assistant Secretary of War Charles Dana said Meade "was totally lacking in cordiality toward those with whom he had business, and in consequence was generally disliked by his subordinates." One compared Meade to "a firecracker, always going bang at somebody near him." General Alexander Webb, on the other hand, did not think Meade's reputation was the result of a bad disposition. In Webb's view, Meade "thought too quick and expected others to think the same without his source of information." Like most officers, Meade had his supporters and detractors.

Meade deeply felt the pressure of his increasing responsibilities. "I sometimes feel very nervous about my position, they are knocking over generals at such a rate." As the Gettysburg campaign began, Major General George Meade had experience as an engineer and a combat officer at brigade, division, and corps levels. The fact that Lee threatened his home state of Pennsylvania also likely further solidified his qualifications to replace Hooker as commander of the Army of the Potomac.

▲ After serving in the Western Theater, Major General Henry Halleck was promoted in July 1862 to general in chief of the Union army. An able administrator, Halleck was ultimately unable to formulate a grand strategy or effectively command armies in the field from his Washington office. Halleck and Hooker disliked each other from their pre-war days in California. Halleck was more supportive of Meade, but his orders were often in the form of suggestions and offered little value. (Library of Congress)

orders to cover both Washington and the garrison at Harpers Ferry. Hooker wanted the latter abandoned, but Halleck refused to approve unless "absolutely necessary." Hooker requested the matter be referred directly to Lincoln and Secretary of War Edwin Stanton. Before receiving a reply, however, Hooker wired Washington on June 27: "I am unable to comply with this condition with the means at my disposal, and earnestly request that I may at once be relieved from the position I occupy." Whether Hooker was bluffing, or truly had enough, Lincoln had little choice but to accept the resignation. Lincoln and the newspapers had been considering alternatives for weeks, with options including John Sedgwick, Pennsylvanians John Reynolds and George Meade, and even the political non-West Pointer Dan Sickles.

Later that evening, a special train departed Washington and headed for Hooker's headquarters at Frederick, Maryland. The train arrived about 1:00 am on June 28. Among the riders was Colonel James Hardie of Henry Halleck's staff. General Sickles, who was returning to the army after a medical leave following Chancellorsville, later complained that Hardie "sat by my side from Washington to Frederick, chatting all the way, without revealing a word of his mission."

back to pre-war clashes in California. Hooker might have been suffering from a concussion inflicted at Chancellorsville. As Lee entered Pennsylvania, Hooker remained unable to gather any meaningful intelligence or articulate a coherent plan.

Hooker erroneously believed that he was likely outnumbered and felt handcuffed by

No One Ever Received a More Important Command

General Hooker's resignation forced another change in command of the Army of the Potomac. As Lee's army penetrated deeper into Pennsylvania, the new Northern commander needed to come up with a plan quickly and bring Lee to battle.

At 3:00 a.m. on June 28 near Frederick, Maryland, Colonel Hardie woke Fifth Corps commander Major General George Meade from his sleep to inform Meade that he had come to "give trouble." Given post-Chancellorsville tensions within the army, Meade's first thought was that he was either to be relieved or arrested. Hardie instead handed him an order from General Halleck placing Meade in command of the Army of the Potomac. Halleck's orders assured Meade that given "the circumstances, no one ever received a more important command."

A "confounded" Meade reportedly "became much agitated" and protested the assignment. According to Hardie, Meade said "half playfully, 'Well, I've been tried and condemned without a hearing, and I suppose I shall have to go to execution.'" Nevertheless, Meade wired his acceptance to Halleck at 7:00 a.m. Despite being "in ignorance of the exact condition of the troops and position of the enemy" Meade determined sensibly to "move toward the Susquehanna, keeping Washington and Baltimore well covered, and if the enemy is checked in his attempt to cross the Susquehanna, or if he turns toward Baltimore, to give him battle."

Travelling to Hooker's nearby headquarters, Hardie then notified Fighting Joe that his resignation had been accepted. Surprised at this news, Hooker "could not wholly mask the revulsion of feeling." A

▼ A monument to George Meade's taking command of the Army of the Potomac stands outside Prospect Hall near Frederick, Maryland. (Robert Housch, Gettysburgdaily.com)

transfer-of-command meeting occurred between Hooker and Meade, with Hardie and Hooker's chief of staff Dan Butterfield also in attendance. Meade was "shocked" to learn of the army's scattered status, to which Hooker "retorted with feeling." The meeting was tense, due to what was later described as "Hooker's chagrin and Meade's overstrung nerves." General Butterfield, despite being a crony of Hooker and hostile to Meade, remained as chief of staff to maintain continuity and because Meade's preferred choices would turn down offers to accept the role over the next few days.

It was uncertain how senior officers would respond to serving under Meade. Some, such as Butterfield or Third Corps commander Sickles, were decidedly Hooker loyalists. Others were certainly frustrated being under Hooker. Frank Haskell, who served on staff in the Second Corps, observed that those who knew Meade "all thought highly of him, a man of great modesty, with none of those qualities, which are noisy and assuming, and hankering for cheap newspaper fame." Among the first to offer Meade congratulations and loyalty assurances was First Corps commander Major General John Reynolds. Meade assured Reynolds that he did not want the job and Reynolds, who had reportedly turned down an offer from Lincoln to assume command, promised Meade his full support.

General Meade inherited an army of more than 93,000 men, in seven infantry corps and one cavalry corps. Meade's first objective was to get the army moving. He decided to move north from Frederick toward Harrisburg with his left and right spread as far as possible to keep Baltimore and Washington covered. This would hopefully halt Lee's advance and bring on a battle "at some point." By June 29, the Army of the Potomac was finally headed toward Pennsylvania. The weather was hot, some roads were dusty, and rounding up numerous drunken stragglers in Frederick was not easy.

▼ The Pennsylvania state capital of Harrisburg was one objective of Lee's invasion. Ewell's Second Corps reached the city's outskirts before being ordered to withdraw to Gettysburg or Cashtown. (James E. Schmick Collection)

June 28 also proved a critical day for the Army of Northern Virginia. Unbeknownst to Lee, J. E. B. Stuart finally crossed the Potomac River at around 3:00 a.m. that morning, after a small engagement at Fairfax Court House the prior day. Upon finally entering Maryland, Stuart called upon the portion of Lee's orders that directed him to inflict damage and gather supplies. Stuart's horsemen entered Rockville, on a key wagon supply road between the Union army and Washington. They tore down miles of telegraph wire and captured at least 125 fully loaded wagons and mule teams. This bounty of supplies proved to be a hindrance to Stuart's advance from here on out. Brief consideration was given toward harassing Washington D.C. before Stuart wisely chose to continue north instead.

Unfortunately, Stuart was not with the vanguard of Lee's advance as Ewell's Second Corps probed deeper into Pennsylvania but stopped short of Harrisburg. Major General Jubal Early's division entered York, and the town leaders surrendered to their occupiers. Brigadier General John B. Gordon's brigade continued toward Wrightsville, but Union militia burned the bridge across the Susquehanna before the Confederates could cross and advance on Harrisburg from that direction. General Ewell bivouacked near Carlisle with the remaining two divisions of his corps, while Jenkins's cavalry foraged and skirmished past Mechanicsburg. Little did they realize that this day brought their final opportunities to plunder Harrisburg and further embarrass Lincoln's war efforts.

Late that evening, a ragged-looking man arrived at General Longstreet's headquarters near Chambersburg. Longstreet had hired Henry Harrison before the army left Virginia to collect intelligence about Hooker's movements.

Harrison returned with information that the enemy had crossed the Potomac, reached Frederick, and was moving northward. Although Longstreet had used Harrison's services previously, staff officers questioned him closely as they knew Lee was not overly fond of civilian scouts. The general would be skeptical of his first real

Meade's Orders

A command turnover while the enemy was deep in Pennsylvania appeared risky, but Hooker left Lincoln and Halleck with no choice. According to Halleck's orders, George Meade would "not be hampered by any minute instructions" and was "free to act as you may deem proper." However, this was contingent on Meade remembering that the Army of the Potomac "is the covering army of Washington ... You will, therefore, maneuver and fight in such a manner as to cover the capital and also Baltimore ... Should General Lee move upon either of these places, it is expected that you will either anticipate him or arrive with him so as to give him battle." Halleck even placed Harpers Ferry—that thorn in Hooker's side—under Meade's direct orders, illustrating the lack of confidence that Washington held in Hooker by this point. Meade was further "authorized to remove from command, and to send from your army, any officer or other person you may deem proper, and to appoint to command as you may deem expedient."

Some might argue that the requirement to cover Washington limited Meade's ability to maneuver, although this was not an unusual constraint. The explicit nature of Halleck's instructions gave Meade a clear understanding of his expectations, and given Lincoln's spotty record in selecting generals, the late stages of an enemy invasion were not the time for creating any uncertainty. Ultimately, the army's movements would be dictated by circumstances on the field and not through Henry Halleck's desk in Washington.

▲ General Lee headquartered at Messersmith's Woods near Chambersburg, Pennsylvania. The woods are long gone, and the site is now surrounded by commercial development. Only a roadside historical marker commemorates the location. (Photo by Tracy Baer)

▶ Brigadier General John Buford's division arrived in Gettysburg on June 30 and opened the battle on the following morning. Buford is credited with fighting a delaying action which gave John Reynolds time to arrive at Gettysburg and deploy infantry, but Buford also provided timely and accurate pre-battle intelligence on the enemy's movements. (Library of Congress)

information on the Army of the Potomac's whereabouts.

Until this point in the campaign, Lee had the initiative and Hooker was the reactionary party. After this, Lee would be the one frequently reacting to his opponent.

Harrison's report forced Lee to modify his operations. While the main component of Harrison's story was accurate since the Yankees were on the move, Lee also concluded that the head of the enemy's column had reached South Mountain and threatened Lee's communications and supply line on the western side. To prevent the Army of the Potomac from moving further west toward the mountains and the valley beyond, Lee decided to concentrate his scattered army east of the mountains. This action would presumably force the Northern commander to also stay on the same side and confront the occupier. Harrison's report was a revelation to Lee because he had heard nothing from his own cavalry. Yet, one of the invasion's primary objectives was to draw the enemy out of Virginia, so the news should not have been too much of an unwelcome surprise.

Lee considered previously concentrating near Chambersburg, west of the mountains.

Profile:
Major General John Reynolds (1820–63)

Major General John Reynolds was born on September 21, 1820, in Lancaster, Pennsylvania. The connected Reynolds family was friends with future President James Buchanan, who nominated Reynolds to West Point. Reynolds graduated in 1841, finishing 26th in his class. After graduation, Reynolds was commissioned a lieutenant in artillery. During the Mexican War, Reynolds served as a 1st lieutenant and was brevetted twice for gallantry.

A lifelong bachelor, Reynolds became engaged to a woman named Catherine "Kate" Hewitt while returning from western postings. They kept their engagement secret, possibly due to religious or social class differences. She was a Catholic and he was a Protestant. War prevented their marriage, and she vowed to join a convent if he were to fall in battle.

From September 1860 to June 1861, Reynolds served as Commandant of Cadets and an instructor at West Point. In August 1861, Reynolds received an appointment as a brigadier general of volunteers in the Union army and put in command of a brigade of the Pennsylvania Reserves. He led his brigade through the Seven Days campaign but embarrassingly was captured while attempting to get some sleep at Gaines' Mill on June 27, 1862. Reynolds was exchanged weeks later and received command of a division of the Pennsylvania Reserves. At Second Manassas, Reynolds led a rear-guard counterattack that bought time for the Union army to escape potential destruction. He missed Antietam because Pennsylvania Governor Andrew Curtin demanded that he command local militia forces during Lee's invasion.

Reynolds assumed command of the First Corps prior to Fredericksburg in late 1862. George Meade led the division of the Pennsylvania Reserves under Reynolds. Meade's division made the only Union breakthrough during the battle, but Reynolds did not reinforce Meade and the attack failed.

After Chancellorsville, President Lincoln met with Reynolds and offered him command of the Army of the Potomac. Reynolds said he declined the offer because Lincoln refused to promise that the government would not interfere in running the army. Since he declined Lincoln's offer, Reynolds retained First Corps command during the Gettysburg campaign.

◀ Major General John Reynolds commanded the First Corps of the Army of the Potomac. General Meade also entrusted Reynolds with the left wing of two additional corps. Reynolds received orders to proceed to Gettysburg on the morning of July 1. His active front-line leadership on McPherson Ridge had significant consequences for the United States Army and for Reynolds personally. (Library of Congress)

▶ General Buford and his devoted staff. Standing to Buford's right (photo left) is Myles Keogh. Buford died of illness in December 1863 while Keogh held him in his arms. Keogh was subsequently killed in 1876 at the battle of Little Big Horn. (Library of Congress)

Longstreet and Hill's corps were already in the vicinity. The decision to concentrate east, however, put everyone in motion. Richard Ewell's corps, as the farthest advance, had the longest distance to travel back. On June 29, Lee's couriers reached Ewell near Carlisle. "I think it preferable to keep on the east side of the mountains," Lee directed. "When you come to Heidlersburg, you can either move directly on Gettysburg or turn down to Cashtown."

Lee's post-battle reports leave room for interpretation regarding Gettysburg or Cashtown as his intended point of concentration. Lee's plans remained fluid based on circumstances, but Gettysburg offered the benefit of a converging road network, easier ability to maneuver or connect with Ewell's scattered corps, was better suited to provide supplies and water, and would keep the Army of the Potomac further away from South Mountain in their pursuit.

As the Army of the Potomac advanced toward Pennsylvania, Brigadier General John Buford's cavalry division received orders to cover and protect the left flank. The Kentucky-born Buford commanded the army's First Division of cavalry. At 37 years old, the career soldier avoided the style and flash that too often accompanied cavalry officers. Buford was described as "straight-forward, honest, conscientious, full of good common sense, and always to be relied on in any emergency." Buford's reconnaissance and dismounted tactics played a crucial role in the battle's opening phases.

The morning of June 30 found the gruff but capable Buford encamped only a few miles north of the Mason–Dixon line, near the village of Fountaindale at Monterey Pass in South Mountain. He was in proximity to a picket line from two Confederate regiments, the 42nd Mississippi and 52nd North Carolina, from Hill's Third Corps. The right of this Confederate picket line stretched toward Lee's main body assembling near Cashtown. "The inhabitants knew of my arrival and the position of the enemy's camp," Buford complained afterward, "yet not one of them gave me a particle of information, nor even mentioned the fact of the enemy's presence. The whole community seemed stampeded, and afraid to speak or to act."

Buford collided with pickets from these units as he began to ride toward Gettysburg that morning. After a brief clash, Buford wisely decided not to risk a larger engagement so far from the remainder of the army and withdrew to Emmitsburg. He reported his observations to First Corps commander John Reynolds and cavalry commander Alfred Pleasonton. After conferring with Reynolds, Buford then headed north up the Emmitsburg Road toward the town of Gettysburg.

Entering his third day on the job, George Meade moved his headquarters to Taneytown, Maryland, on June 30. He directed General Reynolds to assume command of the army's left wing, comprising his own First Corps, Dan Sickles's Third Corps, and Oliver Howard's Eleventh Corps. That morning Reynolds moved his First Corps less than four miles from Emmitsburg toward Marsh Creek and established his own headquarters nearby at Moritz Tavern less than seven miles from the center of Gettysburg.

With conflicting reports that some portion of Lee's army might be near Fairfield, Gettysburg, or moving toward Emmitsburg, Meade and Reynolds corresponded over dispositions on the army's left. "I think if the enemy advances in force from Gettysburg," General

Reynolds opined, "and we are to fight a defensive battle in this vicinity, that the position to be occupied is just north of the town of Emmitsburg," and covering the road to Taneytown.

Meade thought that Buford's presence at Gettysburg should give Reynolds warning if the Confederates advanced either in his direction or on Howard who was moving behind Reynolds toward Emmitsburg. "If, after occupying your present position [Marsh Creek]," Meade wrote Reynolds, "it is your judgment that you would be in better position at Emmitsburg than where you are, you can fall back without waiting for the enemy or further orders. Your present position was given more with a view to an advance on Gettysburg, than a defensive point." As the final day of June 1863 continued, Meade's options were still on the table while he attempted to discern Robert E. Lee's point of concentration.

▲ Major General George Meade established his headquarters at the Benjamin Shunk farm near Taneytown. Meade was located here during the fighting at Gettysburg on July 1. (Photo by Jody Wilson)

The Point of Concentration

The two armies collided at the crossroads town of Gettysburg, Pennsylvania. Lee's attempt to concentrate before bringing on a general engagement and Meade's consideration of a defensive line in Maryland were both scuttled when the two armies finally engaged in battle on the morning of July 1.

James Gettys formally established what became known as Gettysburg in 1786 after he acquired land from his father Samuel and laid out town lots near his father's tavern site. In 1800, Gettysburg became the county seat of the newly created Adams County, ensuring that local government would sustain the town's growth and development. Higher education followed, with the Lutheran Theological Seminary opening its doors in 1826 and Pennsylvania College in 1832. In 1858, construction was completed on a railroad line from Gettysburg to Hanover. By 1860, the town population of approximately 2,400 people supported an economy of carriage manufacturers, tanneries, shoemakers, newspapers, local government, and agriculture on the county's farms.

The surrounding roads drew these two massive armies to Gettysburg in 1863. Ten roads intersected near the center of the town. Coming from every point of the compass, like the spokes of a wheel, troops could access Carlisle or Harrisburg to the

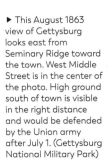

▶ This August 1863 view of Gettysburg looks east from Seminary Ridge toward the town. West Middle Street is in the center of the photo. High ground south of town is visible in the right distance and would be defended by the Union army after July 1. (Gettysburg National Military Park)

north, move west toward the mountains, east to more heavily populated centers such as York or Philadelphia, and south toward Maryland. Some roads such as the Baltimore Pike toward Maryland were improved ("macadamized") for heavier all-weather traffic. In addition, the rolling open countryside allowed for maneuver and observation, while the farms and waterways could sustain large numbers of personnel and animals.

By late June 1863, rumors of an enemy invasion had rippled across the Pennsylvania countryside so many times before that they became old news to the citizenry. Without appreciating how much of war's devastation would soon unfold, the speculation became so common that the people of Adams County joked about it.

On June 26, Gettysburg received its first taste of Lee's invasion when Jubal Early's division approached town and scattered some overmatched local militia. "They came with such horrid yells," Gettysburg resident Sarah Broadhead remembered, "that it was enough to frighten us to death." Broadhead considered them a "miserable looking" bunch and recalled, "how bad I felt to hear them, and to see the traitors' flag floating overhead." Fortunately, Early's visit was short-lived. His men entered town and levied a requisition on the local leaders, but they could not meet the demands. Lee's "Bad Old Man," as Early was known, spared Gettysburg further and instead continued eastward toward York.

The Federal cavalry arrived two days later, on June 28, when Brigadier General Joseph Copeland arrived with portions of his Michigan cavalry brigade. Copeland's own stay was short-lived too, as he received word the following morning that he had been relieved of command. (His successor, a brash young recently promoted brigadier general named George Armstrong Custer, returned with the brigade to fight a few

▼ Modern view of the Cashtown Inn. While in Cashtown, Confederate generals A. P. Hill and Henry Heth made the decision to advance to Gettysburg on July 1. (Author's photo)

▶ James Johnston Pettigrew was a promising young author, lawyer, and soldier. During the Gettysburg campaign, he commanded a brigade in Heth's division. Pettigrew's supply-gathering assignment on June 30 led to his superior officers sending a larger force to Gettysburg on July 1. (W.J. Peele, ed., *Lives of Distinguished North Carolinians with Illustrations and Speeches* [Raleigh, NC: 1898], 413)

days later.) Although the town had been spared, war seemed much more imminent, and tensions were higher.

That excitement had hardly subsided when General Buford arrived at Gettysburg around 11:00 a.m. on June 30 with two brigades of cavalry totaling slightly more than 2,700 men. "Found everybody in a terrible state of excitement," Buford wrote, "on account of the enemy's advance upon this place." As Buford entered town from the south, a body of Confederate infantry approached from the west.

While A. P. Hill's corps concentrated at Cashtown, less than 10 miles to the west, division commander Major General Henry Heth ordered one of his brigades under Brigadier General Johnston Pettigrew to Gettysburg. According to Heth's post-battle report, Pettigrew's mission was to "search the town for army supplies (shoes especially) and return the same day." Heth's post-battle writings set off a long-standing historical debate over the extent to which "shoes" played a part in the Confederate advance to Gettysburg. In later years, Heth likely embellished the significance

of finding footwear and helped perpetuate a myth that shoes caused the battle but searching for "supplies (shoes especially)" was consistent with the invasion's supply-gathering objectives.

General Buford reported his arrival as "just in time to meet the enemy entering the town, and in good season to drive him back before his getting a foothold." Actually, Pettigrew withdrew his brigade back to Cashtown because he was unsure of the enemy's strength and had received no orders to fight. Buford's men spent the remainder of the day reconnoitering the region and interviewing locals. By nightfall, he had an assessment that "Hill's corps is massed just back of Cashtown … Ewell's corps is crossing the mountains from Carlisle … Longstreet, from all I can learn, is still behind Hill." Buford deployed videttes (or sentries) on a seven-mile front from Fairfield Road to the Harrisburg Road, including along Chambersburg Pike in the direction from which Pettigrew had approached and withdrawn.

That evening at Cashtown, Confederate generals Hill, Heth, and Pettigrew conferred over the meaning of the day's activities. According to Heth's recollections, General Hill had just returned from a conference with Lee, where reports indicated the enemy was still as far south as Middleburg. Hill opined that the forces at Gettysburg likely were a "detachment of observation" and not a significant force.

General James Johnston Pettigrew hailed from a wealthy North Carolina family and was only days short of what would be his 35th and final birthday on July 4. President Jefferson Davis was among those who recognized Pettigrew's potential and abilities, although he was not a professional military man (despite also being a scholar, author, lawyer, and politician). Pettigrew had combat experience, including being wounded and captured at Seven Pines in the summer of 1862. When he returned, however, he received a new brigade and spent the fall 1862–winter 1863 in North Carolina and Virginia away from Lee's army. In late May 1863, his brigade joined the Army of Northern Virginia and Henry Heth's division.

It has been speculated that factors such as Pettigrew's non-Virginia bloodline, non-professional military status, and his new arrival in Lee's army caused Hill and Heth to simply discredit his report. Lieutenant Louis Young on Pettigrew's staff wrote that Pettigrew could not convince his superiors that they had observed more than simply emergency call-ups. "This spirit of unbelief had taken such hold, that I doubt if any of the commanders of the brigades, except General Pettigrew, believed that they were marching to battle." The post-battle reports of Heth, Hill, and Lee all indicated, however, that they believed the enemy's force to be primarily cavalry. Hill then sent couriers to Lee and Ewell informing both that he intended to advance on Gettysburg early tomorrow and "discover what was in my front." Skeptical or not, Heth would move forward on July 1 with a full division of nearly 7,500 men and artillery. If June 30 was a supply-gathering mission, July 1 was not.

In addition to Buford's assessment of Lee's position, George Meade received an additional late-night message from engineer Herman Haupt confirming that Lee was falling back from Harrisburg, York, and Carlisle with an apparent concentration near Chambersburg. These reports changed Meade's plans for July 1. He had initially intended to move toward Hanover, Pennsylvania, and the rail hub at Hanover Junction to open communication with Baltimore for supplies. The confirmation of Lee's withdrawal from

◄ Herman Haupt was a civil engineer and railroad construction engineer. Haupt revolutionized railroad military transportation for the Union army during the Civil War. His message late on June 30 helped inform George Meade that Lee's army was withdrawing from the Harrisburg vicinity. (Library of Congress)

the Susquehanna region satisfied Meade that his own northward movements had relieved Harrisburg. Meade determined it "was no longer his intention to assume the offensive until the enemy's movements or position should render such an operation certain of success."

Marching orders for July 1 had already been issued, however, for Reynolds's First Corps to go to Gettysburg and Howard's Eleventh Corps also to Gettysburg "or supporting distance." Those two officers spent the evening of June 30 at Reynolds's Moritz Tavern headquarters reviewing maps and communications. Howard later wrote that Reynolds appeared depressed. The marching orders had not yet arrived when Howard departed for Emmitsburg at 11:00 p.m. and both officers turned in for a night's sleep.

As late as 7:00 a.m. on July 1, Meade wrote Halleck, "The point of Lee's concentration and the nature of the country, when ascertained, will determine whether I attack him or not." Meade considered both offensive and defensive options, but only after confirming Lee's withdrawal from the

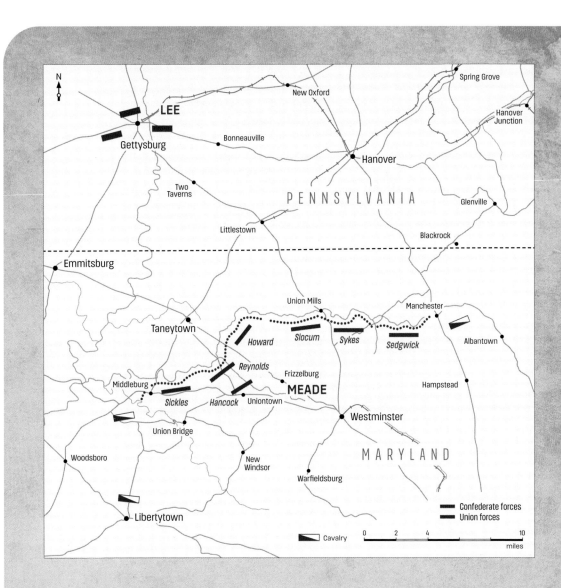

▲ Meade's proposed Pipe Creek Line.

Harrisburg area late on June 30 did Meade issue orders considering formation of a defensive position to await Lee's attack.

Among options on the table was a defensive line along Pipe Creek in Maryland. Scouted by Meade's engineers and his chief of artillery during the preceding days, Meade's Pipe Creek line incorporated the defensive benefits of the terrain but also covered roads that Lee's army might utilize to threaten Baltimore or Washington. Yet, this was not really a continuous "battle line" as it was more than 17 miles in length from Middleburg on the left to Manchester on the right. Robert E. Lee was unlikely to attack along such an extended front, but by covering the necessary roads, Meade could hopefully concentrate wherever Lee threatened.

The subsequent issuing order, dubbed the "Pipe Creek Circular," was not distributed until sometime on July 1. Although brilliant in design, the execution would have required Lee to bring his army back into Maryland and willingly engage Meade's entrenched forces. Meade's own description of the circular emphasized it as a preliminary order "issued by me before I was aware that the enemy had crossed the mountain, and that there was any collision between the two forces [at Gettysburg]. That preliminary order was intended as an order of maneuver, based upon contingencies which did not occur, and therefore the order was not executed." Although never executed, historians continue to debate the Pipe Creek Circular's importance to July 1 dispositions, in part because Meade's enemies attempted later to use this "preliminary order" to portray the commander as unwilling to fight at Gettysburg. Such were the benefits of commanding the Army of the Potomac.

Since the Pipe Creek Circular was not issued until July 1, some of Meade's corps commanders received it and some did not. Among those who likely did not receive it was John Reynolds. The circular would have placed him and his left wing near Middleburg. Yet, Reynolds continued to operate under the June 30 orders (which he did not receive until early July 1) to march his First Corps to Gettysburg, more than 15 miles from Middleburg.

Meade also continued to issue messages to Reynolds that morning. "The commanding general cannot decide whether it is his best policy to move to attack until he learns something more definite of the point at which the enemy is concentrating." Meade confirmed that Reynolds's orders to go to Gettysburg were issued "before positive knowledge of the enemy's withdrawal from Harrisburg" was received. Although Meade acknowledged that Gettysburg was "not at first glance" a strategic point to concentrate his own army, he also expressed insufficient acquaintance with the vicinity to judge it for either an offensive or defensive position. Feeling Reynolds was better situated to assess the terrain, Meade acknowledged that he "would gladly receive from you any suggestions" on those points. Subsequent events prevented Reynolds from providing these suggestions, but it demonstrates further that Meade was not locked into a defensive posture on Pipe Creek, nor did Reynolds receive instructions to execute the circular.

A staff officer woke Reynolds at 4:00 a.m. that morning with the orders for the day. Around 6:00 a.m. a note arrived from Howard at Emmitsburg stating that he would follow within supporting distance. Between 7:00 and 8:00 a.m., Reynolds summoned division commander Major General Abner Doubleday to the Moritz Tavern. Since Reynolds commanded the left wing, Doubleday temporarily led the First Corps. Reynolds informed Doubleday that he had already given orders to Brigadier General James Wadsworth's division and Captain James Hall's battery to move forward. Reynolds would accompany Wadsworth while Doubleday was to bring up the balance of the corps.

It was only about seven miles from Moritz Tavern to the center of Gettysburg, and less to the southern outskirts. Some of Reynolds's aides recalled afterwards that he seemed to be in good spirits, apparently lifting the depression that Howard observed the prior evening. Reynolds told Colonel Charles Wainwright of the First Corps Artillery Brigade that he did not expect a fight today, but the corps was only moving up to be within support of Buford, who would then push out from Gettysburg.

According to General Wadsworth, Reynolds was "generally very particular in communicating his orders to his division, but on that occasion he communicated none, if he had any." Meade and Reynolds had discussed in recent days the potential to fight north of Emmitsburg in the event of an attack in force, but Reynolds communicated no such intent to any key subordinate while on the march. Circumstances would dictate subsequent actions.

From Cashtown, after having decided to "advance the next morning and discover what was in my front," A. P. Hill ordered Henry Heth's division to advance toward Gettysburg along the Chambersburg Pike. Heth departed around 5:00 a.m. with his four infantry brigades and artillery in Major William Pegram's battalion.

Major General Henry "Harry" Heth was 37 years old. A product of old Virginia stock, Heth traced his lineage to the Revolution and was a cousin of fellow-Virginian George Pickett. The cousins shared the distinction of both being last in their class at West Point. Heth received that honor in 1847. Heth's close friend and senior officer at Gettysburg A. P. Hill was also in the same class after repeating a year due to medical reasons.

Early in the Civil War, Heth served briefly as General Lee's quartermaster in the Virginia Provisional Army. Heth was gregarious and likeable, but also opinionated. Even General Lee was not immune to Heth's charms. Heth was said to be the only subordinate whom Lee called by his first name. Heth's first two years of the war were spent primarily in Western Virginia and East Tennessee. In early 1863, Lee lobbied for Heth to join the Army of Northern Virginia. He immediately became the senior brigadier in his friend Hill's Light Division.

▼ Major General Henry Heth was a friend of Robert E. Lee's and promoted to division command after Chancellorsville. Heth sent his division to Gettysburg on the morning of July 1 as a reconnaissance-in-force to see what enemy were there. Heth is often blamed for accidentally starting the battle, but his superior officer General Hill authorized the movement, and Lee's orders to "avoid a general engagement" quickly became impossible once contact was made. (Library of Congress)

Heth's first large-scale battle experience occurred at Chancellorsville. Dorsey Pender received most of the division when Hill was promoted to Third Corps command. Lee and Hill did not forget Heth, however, as they created a new division for their mutual friend. He received a promotion to major general in May 1863. Like many other officers at Gettysburg, Heth entered the battle with little or no combat experience at this level.

Brigadier General James Archer's small brigade of fewer than 1,200 men led the way for Heth's division. Archer's slight build and "pretty" features had dubbed him "Sally" while attending Princeton University, but he was considered "every inch a soldier" by his men. Behind Archer was the 2,300-man brigade under inexperienced Brigadier General Joseph Davis, who was the nephew of Confederate President Jefferson Davis. Despite no available cavalry to screen the march, Heth did not deploy skirmishers for most of the movement. It may have been because much of the ground east of Cashtown was already behind Confederate skirmish lines, or because Heth simply did not expect to run into opposition.

By all indications, with a full division and artillery, Hill and Heth were performing a reconnaissance-in-force to discover or test the enemy's strength. Among those who later wrote with the certainty of hindsight, Lee's staff officer Walter Taylor indicated that Heth was to ascertain what was in his front and if enemy infantry were discovered,

▲ Brigadier General James Archer's brigade led Heth's movements on July 1. The 45-year-old Maryland native was slight of build but cited for bravery during the Mexican War and had capably led his brigade since June 1862. After being captured at Gettysburg, Archer remained a prisoner of war until the summer of 1864. Captivity wrecked his already frail health, and he died in October 1864. (Library of Congress)

◄ The home of local blacksmith Ephraim Wisler was located on the Chambersburg Pike at Knoxlyn Ridge. A vidette post from the 8th Illinois Cavalry fired what is credited as the battle's opening shot from Wisler's property. (Gettysburg National Military Park)

▶ The veterans argued amongst themselves over who deserved credit for firing the first shot. Lieutenant Marcellus Jones and friends cemented their claim by having this shaft erected on the spot where Jones said he opened the battle. Compared to when this image was taken, considerably more overgrowth exists behind the monument today. (Gettysburg National Military Park)

he was to report immediately but "without forcing an engagement." How Heth would avoid an engagement is unclear. His entire division, with Major General Dorsey Pender's soon to follow, was bottlenecked along one road should they encounter hostile forces. General Heth later reminded his superiors that he was "ignorant what force was at or near Gettysburg, and supposed it consisted of cavalry, most probably supported by a brigade or two of infantry." By approximately 7:30 a.m., Archer's lead elements covered roughly four miles as they approached Marsh Creek. A single shot rang out.

This shot came from a vidette post almost 800 yards away, manned by members of the 8th Illinois Cavalry in Colonel William Gamble's brigade of Buford's division. This outpost was located along the pike and next to the home of local blacksmith Ephraim Wisler. A handful of Federal cavalrymen were observing Heth's advance when Private George Sager raised his single-shot carbine to fire at a Confederate officer on a horse near the Marsh Creek bridge. Lieutenant Marcellus

Jones stopped him. "Hold on, George, give me the honor of opening this ball." Jones then borrowed a carbine, rested it on a fence rail and took what has been officially credited as the opening shot of the battle of Gettysburg. Others along Buford's extended picket line also claimed to have fired "first shots" earlier than Marcellus Jones that morning, but it was this action along the Chambersburg Pike that truly signaled the opening of the main battle.

After a brief halt, General Archer's brigade of Alabamians and Tennesseans finally deployed skirmishers and pushed forward again. Meanwhile, a gun from Marye's Fredericksburg battery unlimbered near the Samuel Lohr farm and opened fire from about a quarter mile west of Marsh Creek, much to the chagrin of a nearby resident who yelled, "My God, you are not going to fire here are you?" One of the artillery shells supposedly landed in front of Ephraim Wisler who had come out of his house to see all the excitement. He was reportedly so shocked and "prostrated" by the experience that he took to his bed and died about a month later.

John Buford's cavalry videttes were not expected to stand up and fight an entire division of infantry. The cavalrymen on both sides of the Chambersburg Pike fell back slowly and bought time as they slowed Archer and Davis. Firing while dismounted and with their reserves thrown in, they now numbered perhaps 200 men, with every fourth man pulled off the line to hold their horses. Over the next two hours, Buford's men fell back slightly less than two miles, over Herr Ridge, down across the banks of Willoughby's Run, and joined Gamble's main line on McPherson Ridge. (This ridge was named after a farm situated there and owned by Edward McPherson.)

"Our skirmishers, fighting under cover of trees and fences," Colonel Gamble reported afterwards, "were sharply engaged, did good execution, and retarded the progress of the enemy as much as could possibly be expected." This was not a slugfest but a skirmish; casualties were light on both sides. Confederate recollections often attached little significance to the delay, while Buford's veterans proudly recalled forcing their opponents to fight for "every inch of ground." The cavalrymen did what tactics called for. Buford slowed

◄ Colonel William Gamble was a 45-year-old Irish immigrant who commanded one of the brigades in Buford's division. Gamble was on medical leave and missed Brandy Station, where the officer temporarily commanding his brigade was killed. Gamble returned to the army in mid-June. Heth's division marched into Gamble's vidette line on the morning of July 1. (Library of Congress)

Heth's advance into Gettysburg until Reynolds could reach the field.

As John Reynolds and his First Corps column approached Gettysburg along the Emmitsburg Road, the sounds of battle became progressively louder. The pace quickened. Reynolds met one of Buford's staffers about three miles south of town who confirmed the fighting along the Chambersburg Pike. Reynolds and some staff officers quickly rode ahead of their foot soldiers into the town, and after

◄ Chambersburg Pike looking west with Herr Ridge in background. The Confederates advanced toward the camera against Union defenders in the foreground for most of the day. Photo taken circa 1903. (Gettysburg National Military Park)

▲ The Lutheran Seminary's original building stands as a significant Gettysburg landmark. General Buford's signal officer Lieutenant Aaron Jerome utilized the building's cupola as an observation post. The building served afterwards as one of Gettysburg's largest field hospitals. This 1863 image shows the town-facing east side of the building. (Library of Congress)

▼ A view from the Lutheran Seminary cupola looking southeast toward Gettysburg. Cemetery Hill is visible in the distance. Photo taken circa 1878–83. (New York Public Library Digital Collections)

receiving directions from some residents, they approached the grounds of the Lutheran Theological Seminary.

Lieutenant Aaron Jerome occupied a signal station in the cupola of the Lutheran Seminary. The view from this elevated structure provided Buford's signal officer with the ability to gather intelligence of Confederate troop movements. General Buford joined him. According to Jerome, as Buford's outnumbered forces were in danger of being driven back, the lieutenant scanned in the direction of Emmitsburg when he saw a friendly force approximately two miles away. He soon recognized the colors of the First Corps. The details of this meeting between Reynolds and Buford are debated and have been heavily romanticized. In one of Jerome's versions, General Reynolds and his staff officers arrived at a gallop as Reynolds inquired "How things were going on?" Buford was still in the cupola and gave a "characteristic answer, 'Let's go and see.'"

Reynolds arrived on the field at approximately 10:00 a.m. as Archer, Davis, and Pegram's artillery reached Herr Ridge. This was Heth's last chance to avoid a "general engagement." Near this prominent ridge, less than one mile west of the fledgling Union position on McPherson Ridge, Archer deployed his brigade to the Confederate right on the south side of the pike while Davis's men filed left onto the north side. Pettigrew and Brockenbrough's brigades remained behind them. As many as 17 guns in Pegram's battalion deployed on Herr Ridge to support Heth's attack.

As the two sides prepared to exchange fire, the Southern artillerists outnumbered the six 3-inch Ordnance rifles in Buford's only available battery under 21-year-old Lieutenant John Calef. Buford directed Calef to spread the battery's three sections out to give the impression of greater strength. Two sections unlimbered on opposite sides of the Chambersburg Pike, while the third unlimbered further south along McPherson Ridge. At one point, Calef found Buford sitting on his horse, calmly smoking his pipe. "Our men are in

a pretty hot pocket, but, my boy, we must hold this position until the infantry comes up." Calef observed a "double line of battle gray" at less than 1,000 yards' distance and had his men open fire. One of Calef's rifles, number 233, is credited with firing the first Union artillery shot of the battle.

After conferring with Buford along McPherson Ridge, Reynolds selected Captain Stephen Weld to carry an urgent message to Meade in Taneytown. Weld arrived at army headquarters shortly before 11:30 a.m. Reynolds reported, "the enemy are advancing in strong force, and that I fear they will get to the heights beyond the town before I can." Reynolds promised further to "fight them inch by inch" and barricade the streets if driven into the town to "hold them back as long as possible." Meade appeared pleased by Reynolds's commitment. "Good! That is just like Reynolds; he will hold on to the bitter end."

The matter of what "heights" Reynolds referred to is open for debate, but he committed to defending McPherson Ridge west of town. Reynolds rode back

▼ Modern view from the Lutheran Seminary cupola looking west toward McPherson Ridge. The visible tree lines were considerably thinner in 1863. (Rob Williams, Seminary Ridge Museum and Education Center)

▲ A Mathew Brady image taken only days after the battle. Brady (wearing the hat) is looking southeast into Herbst Woods. The Lutheran Seminary cupola is visible in the distance. Note the lack of undergrowth in the woods as compared to today. (Library of Congress)

▶ Major General Abner Doubleday was a career officer in the United States Army. He inherited the July 1 fighting west of Gettysburg after Reynolds's death. History best remembers him as being the inventor of baseball, which is something he did not do. (Library of Congress)

or brigade commander than the wing commander of three corps, he selected a position for Hall's battery and ordered the captain to engage the enemy's guns on Herr Ridge. He then ordered Wadsworth to support Hall's right and Reynolds promised to protect the left. Captain Hall recalled later that Reynolds was "extremely anxious, saying to Gen. Wadsworth in the exact following language, 'General, move a strong infantry support immediately to Hall's right for he is my defender until I can get the troops now coming up into line.'"

Three of Cutler's regiments—the 76th New York, 56th Pennsylvania, and 147th New York—moved to Hall's right and to the north side of the Chambersburg Pike. There they awaited Joe Davis's approach. General Cutler assured the colonel of the 56th Pennsylvania that Davis's approaching troops were enemy soldiers, and the regiment opened fire. This is considered the first infantry volley fired by the Army of the Potomac during the battle.

Meanwhile, the other two regiments present from Cutler's brigade, the 84th New York (also designated the 14th Brooklyn) and the 95th New York, were split into what has been called a "demi-brigade" and posted south of the pike. Reynolds also spoke to Colonel Edward Fowler of the 84th New York. Shortly thereafter, Archer's brigade opened fire on Fowler's men.

General Abner Doubleday oversaw the arrival of the First Corps's other two divisions onto the field. Doubleday commanded the Third Division in First Corps since early 1863. The 44-year-old Doubleday was a West Point graduate and career United States Army officer. His most notable experience prior to Gettysburg was firing the first cannon shot in defense of Fort Sumter during the opening battle of the Civil War. The New York native subsequently was

to hurry Wadsworth's leading division forward. According to Wadsworth, after a momentary consultation, Reynolds decided "if we went into the town the enemy would shell it and destroy it, and that we had better take a position in front of the town." A fence gap was created on the west side of the Emmitsburg Road, near Nicholas Codori's farm, and the First Corps cut across the fields toward Seminary Ridge beyond. Brigadier General Lysander Cutler's brigade led the way and was then followed by Captain James Hall's battery.

General Reynolds seemed to be everywhere. Acting more like a division

referred to as the "Hero of Sumter," a term sometimes applied with sarcasm.

Despite military experience dating back to the 1840s, and capable performances at some battles such as Antietam, Doubleday seems to have been considered mediocre at best; as a general he inspired little confidence. George Meade once joked that he was happy Doubleday had taken command of Meade's old division because the men "will think a great deal more of me than before." This lack of confidence might partially explain the number of dispositions made by Reynolds personally without Doubleday early on July 1.

Hearing the combat, Doubleday pressed ahead of his men toward McPherson Ridge. Reynolds was occupied posting Cutler's men, but a staff officer returned with instructions for Doubleday to cover the left of the First Corps position. This would have Doubleday defending the Fairfield (also referred to as the Hagerstown) Road, which was not yet threatened, while Reynolds continued to be extraordinarily hands-on and supervised

the Chambersburg Pike on the right. The McPherson Ridge position would prove later to be of dubious defensive value, but the fast-acting Reynolds ensured that the two roads entering Gettysburg from the west received coverage.

The other brigade in Wadsworth's division, the famed "Black Hats" of the Iron Brigade under Brigadier General Solomon Meredith, had just reached Seminary Ridge and headed toward McPherson Ridge. An 18-acre woodlot owned by Edward McPherson's neighbor John Herbst dominated the ridgeline south of McPherson's property. General Archer's Confederates were beginning to infiltrate the western side of these woods and potentially threatened Reynolds's fledgling position. One of Reynolds's staff officers hurried along Meredith's lead regiment, the 2nd Wisconsin. They were hit by a volley from Archer's men as they moved into line and double-quicked toward the eastern end of Herbst Woods.

General Reynolds remained mounted and behind the 2nd Wisconsin. Urging

▼ General Reynolds's death at the outskirts of Herbst Woods. Engraving based on sketch from artist Alfred Waud. (Library of Congress)

▼ A small monument
was dedicated in 1886
to commemorate the
approximate site where
General Reynolds fell.
(Author's photo)

them forward, the general shouted, "Forward men, forward for God's sake, and drive those fellows out of the woods!" He then looked backward toward the Lutheran Seminary, to check probably on the progress of the rest of the Iron Brigade.

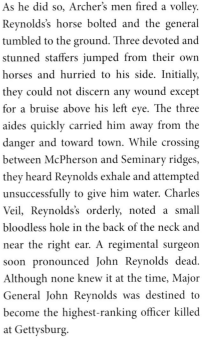

As he did so, Archer's men fired a volley. Reynolds's horse bolted and the general tumbled to the ground. Three devoted and stunned staffers jumped from their own horses and hurried to his side. Initially, they could not discern any wound except for a bruise above his left eye. The three aides quickly carried him away from the danger and toward town. While crossing between McPherson and Seminary ridges, they heard Reynolds exhale and attempted unsuccessfully to give him water. Charles Veil, Reynolds's orderly, noted a small bloodless hole in the back of the neck and near the right ear. A regimental surgeon soon pronounced John Reynolds dead. Although none knew it at the time, Major General John Reynolds was destined to become the highest-ranking officer killed at Gettysburg.

General Reynolds's early exit occurred before he communicated any plan to General Doubleday beyond defending the ridgeline. While Meade and Reynolds had discussed falling back toward Emmitsburg if attacked by overwhelming force on the prior day, that was before Reynolds had arrived at Gettysburg. Reynolds expressed no such intent during the march to Gettysburg or during his brief time on the battlefield. Likewise, Reynolds did not receive Meade's Pipe Creek communication to withdraw to Middleburg before being struck down. Finally, neither Doubleday nor any senior officer on the field expressed any understanding that they were supposed to fall back into Maryland at this stage. "General Reynolds' intention appeared to be simply to defend the two roads entering the town from the northwest and southwest," Doubleday wrote afterward, "and to occupy and hold the woods between them."

The remainder of the Iron Brigade joined the 2nd Wisconsin on McPherson Ridge and the east side of Herbst Woods. This brigade was distinctive geographically, by reputation, and in appearance. With about 1,800 men in total, these were units from what was then the western United States. To the 2nd Wisconsin's left formed the 7th Wisconsin, 19th Indiana, and 24th Michigan. Behind them in reserve for the moment was the 6th Wisconsin. Their "Iron Brigade" nickname originated at South Mountain in 1862 when an impressed General George McClellan observed, "They must be made of iron." They often wore black 1858 Hardee hats, rather than the blue kepis worn by most other regiments, earning them the "Black Hats" as another nickname. Brigadier General Solomon Meredith, dubbed "Long Sol" due to his 6'7" height, commanded the brigade at Gettysburg. Meredith benefitted from political connections and some, such as his predecessor General John Gibbon, protested that Meredith received brigade command for political reasons at the expense of other more-qualified candidates.

General Meredith's brigade squared off against Archer's (left to right) 7th Tennessee, 14th Tennessee, 1st Tennessee,

and 13th Alabama. If Heth's men had only expected to fight some Yankee cavalry, then they were surprised to see the "Black Hats" confronting them. As the Southerners climbed the eastern bank of Willoughby's Run, fighting became increasingly close quarters. Smoke and the terrain concealed movements on both sides. As Archer's Tennessee regiments fought in front of Herbst Woods, the 13th Alabama on the brigade's right received orders to wheel left toward the woods. Unfortunately, in doing so they were outflanked by the 19th Indiana and 24th Michigan as those units entered the fight.

The Iron Brigade's left-positioned regiments charged Archer's men. Some Southerners surrendered immediately, while others attempted to escape across

▲ The Iron Brigade monuments are distinguishable by having the brigade's five-sided symbol on their tops. The 2nd Wisconsin, pictured here, also includes the circle symbol of the First Corps, a relief of the brigade's black hats, and pink granite. (Author's photo)

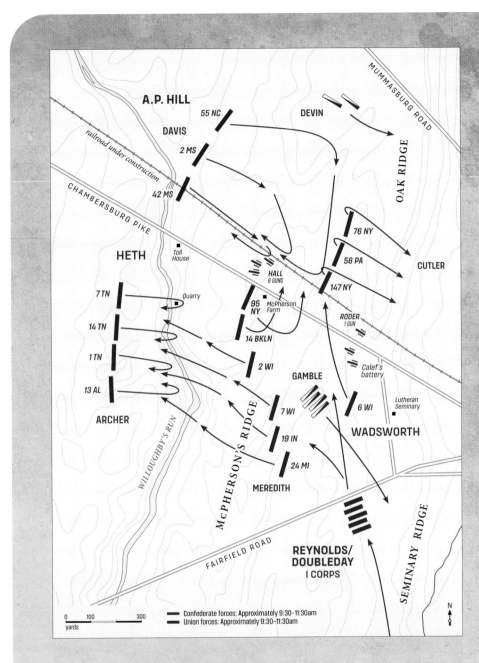

▲ July 1 morning action north and south of Chambersburg Pike.

Willoughby's Run as Yankee pursuers splashed behind them. Early accounts exaggerated the number of captured prisoners as being as high as 1,500 men. More realistic estimates show Archer's brigade lost about 684 men for the entire battle (including the July 3 action) and slightly less than 400 missing/captured.

General Archer found himself among those captured. Private Patrick Maloney of the 2nd Wisconsin grabbed Archer about 30 yards west of Willoughby's Run and wrestled the diminutive officer into submission. While sullenly trudging to the rear, old colleague Abner Doubleday greeted the vanquished Archer. "Good morning, Archer! How are you? I am glad to see you!" Archer replied less favorably. "Well, I am not glad to see you by a damn sight."

James Archer became the first general officer captured during Lee's command of the Army of Northern Virginia, an omen that things might not be as easy for Lee's army going forward. Archer remained in captivity until the summer of 1864 when he briefly rejoined the army. His health was ruined, however, and he died in October 1864. Yet, Archer fared better than Private

Maloney, his captor. Maloney was killed later that same day.

While Meredith went into action south of Chambersburg Pike, the majority of Cutler's brigade ran into trouble north of

▲ Brigadier General Lysander Cutler held multiple occupations prior to the Civil War. He was a businessman, teacher, politician, and pioneer. A tenacious fighter, Cutler started the war as colonel of the 6th Wisconsin and might have led the Iron Brigade were it not for Solomon Meredith's political connections. (Library of Congress)

◄ A modern view of General Cutler's battle line north of the railroad cut bridge. The camera is looking southeast with Cutler's regimental monuments visible on Reynolds Avenue. The 76th New York on Cutler's right is the monument closest to the camera. The Confederates attacked from camera right to left. (Photo by Phil Spaugy)

the roadway. The 56-year-old Brigadier General Lysander Cutler was a former colonel of the 6th Wisconsin and had been General John Gibbon's choice to take command of the Iron Brigade in 1862 before the politically connected Solomon Meredith received that assignment instead. Cutler received a promotion to brigadier general in November 1862 and obtained brigade command in the First Corps in March 1863. Not necessarily popular with his men, Cutler was called "rugged as a wolf" by one soldier. Cutler saw little action at Chancellorsville, so Gettysburg became his first real opportunity to lead his own brigade in action. Five of his six regiments arrived at Gettysburg on July 1 for a total strength of less than 1,600 men.

While Cutler's 56th Pennsylvania fired some of the battle's opening salvos north of the Chambersburg Pike, other units in the brigade struggled to get in line. The 76th

New York was slower to deploy on the right, due to incoming artillery fire and a volley from the 55th North Carolina which was barreling down on Cutler's exposed right. Major Andrew Gover, the New Yorkers' commander, was originally unsure if the troops to his right front were friend or foe and he initially hesitated returning fire. Finally, the 147th New York was cut off from the brigade when Hall's battery unlimbered on the north side of the Chambersburg Pike, and they briefly stopped near the McPherson buildings. As a result, the New Yorkers were initially not on the brigade line's left, and this caused Cutler's flanks— the left of the 56th Pennsylvania and right of the 76th New York—to be in the air in the unsheltered countryside.

An unfinished railroad cut also sat between the Pennsylvanians' left and the right of Hall's battery. This railroad embankment was dug in the 1830s,

▼ Modern view of the railroad cut looking west. The bridge and railroad tracks are post-battle, and grading for the bridge added elevation to the ridgeline. Non-historic vegetation spoils the view toward the 6th Wisconsin and 95th New York regimental monuments on the left. (Author's photo)

heading west from Gettysburg parallel to the Chambersburg Pike, but was not completed when funding was cut off. No tracks were laid, but the abandoned railroad remained and served as a wagon road strewn with boulders, dirt, and stone. In the excitement of deploying his guns, Captain Hall did not realize that this cut was only about 20 yards from his right piece.

General Cutler's deployment was only part of his problem. Opposing Cutler's men, and closing in on them, were three of Davis's regiments of the 55th North Carolina (on the left), 2nd Mississippi, and 42nd Mississippi. At about 1,700 men, they significantly outnumbered Cutler's isolated three regiments of about 1,000 men. Seeing the opportunity, the 55th North Carolina's Colonel John Connally wheeled his regiment towards the New Yorkers' exposed right. Connally then grabbed his regiment's colors in an extra attempt to urge his men forward. This drew gunfire which wounded the colonel. A major inquired if Connally's wounds were bad and the colonel replied, "Yes, but do not pay attention to me; take the colors and keep ahead of the Mississippians."

As Cutler described the action afterwards, he found himself "engaged with a vastly superior force of the enemy, advancing in two lines, at short range, in front and on my right flank." He also made a point of noting that Reynolds had detached his other two regiments (the so-called demi-brigade) further to the left and south of the pike. "The three regiments under my immediate command fought as only brave men can fight, and held their ground until ordered to fall back, by General Wadsworth, to the woods on the next ridge." The 56th Pennsylvania and 76th New York retreated as ordered to the woods behind their position, but this

◀ Brigadier General Joseph Davis was the 38-year-old nephew of Confederate President Jefferson Davis. General Davis had no formal military training and had been a lawyer and politician prior to the war. His commission as a brigadier general was approved only after open criticism about nepotism and an initial rejection by the Confederate Senate. (Warner, *Generals in Gray*, 68)

left the 147th New York and Hall's battery alone against Davis's three regiments.

After their brief halt near the McPherson buildings, Lieutenant Colonel Francis Miller's 147th New York crossed the pike to support Hall's battery. The New Yorkers advanced over a shallow end of the railroad cut before turning to face their attackers from the 42nd Mississippi. Miller's men positioned themselves in a wheatfield and traded blows with the Mississippians. Yet, they were now in danger from Davis's three regiments after the rest of Cutler's men retired. Since they were several hundred yards in front of the rest of the brigade, it took longer for Wadsworth's retreat order to reach Miller. Unfortunately, Miller was shot in the head before he could relay the order to his men. Major George Harney took command and continued to fight while unaware of the order. General Wadsworth then sent a second courier to the regiment with orders to fall back. Major Harney told his men to drop excess equipment except for ammunition and cartridge boxes. "In retreat, double-quick, run!" The New Yorkers dashed eastward toward Seminary

Ridge and property owned by local widow Mary Thompson.

The opening fighting consumed roughly 30 minutes, but General Cutler was unhappy with the morning's developments. He admonished one of the 147th's officers: "You have lost your colors, sir!" To which the man pointed proudly to the color guard coming off field. "General, the 147th never loses its colors." Cutler apologized. "Boys, I'll take it all back. It was just like cock-fighting today. We fight a little and run a little. There are no supports."

While Cutler's retreat seemed justified, it unfortunately left Captain Hall's battery alone on this part of the field with three enemy regiments. Hall's six 3-inch rifles had been exchanging shot and shell with Confederate artillery on Herr Ridge for about 25 minutes when Davis's threat first appeared. As the Mississippians were at times only 60 yards from his right piece, Hall turned his center and right sections to hit them with canister. Hall considered the canister very effective when "to my surprise I saw my support falling back without any order having been given me to retire. Feeling that if the position was too advanced for infantry it was equally so for artillery, I ordered the battery to retire by sections, although having no order to do so." Pursued by their opponents as they retreated toward Seminary Ridge, Hall lost one of his cannons when it got stuck at a fence gap and the Confederates shot and bayoneted all the horses.

Cutler and Hall's departures left Davis's men as temporary masters of the field north of the Chambersburg Pike. South of the pike, the Iron Brigade's 6th Wisconsin under Lieutenant Colonel Rufus Dawes intended to take position on one of the brigade's flanks. Dawes received orders to hold a position in the swale between McPherson and Seminary ridges. Not long after, a lieutenant on Doubleday's staff arrived with orders to move to the right since Cutler's regiments were falling back. Dawes formed his approximately 320-man regiment along with about 100 more men who had been detached as the brigade's reserves. They headed north in the swale toward the Chambersburg Pike. A member of General Meredith's staff accompanied Dawes and shouted, "Go like hell! It looks as though they are driving Cutler."

At this stage, Davis's men were pursuing Cutler and Hall off the field, so Lieutenant Colonel Dawes deployed his regiment facing the pike and toward the enemy's exposed right flank. Dawes's horse suddenly reared and plunged as it was struck by an enemy bullet. The colonel was thrown to the ground in front of his men, who replied with what Dawes remembered as a "hearty cheer" while he quickly recovered and proceeded on foot. The regiment reached the fence on the south side of the pike and opened fire. The Mississippians and North Carolinians abandoned their pursuit of Cutler and Hall by taking cover in the unfinished railroad cut that ran parallel to

▶ Lieutenant Colonel Rufus Dawes served with the Iron Brigade and came from an illustrious family. His great-grandfather William Dawes alerted colonial minutemen of the British army's approach prior to the battles of Lexington and Concord. Rufus Dawes fathered four nationally known sons, including Charles Dawes who served as vice president of the United States from 1925 to 1929. (Rufus Dawes, *Service with the Sixth Wisconsin Volunteers* [Marietta, OH, 1890], 257)

Dawes's line. The Yankees were unaware of the cut and to them it briefly appeared as if the ground had simply swallowed up the Confederates!

General Davis's men were now firing from inside the railroad cut, while the 6th Wisconsin climbed fences on both sides of the Chambersburg Pike and advanced across the road. Approximately 130 yards of open ground stood between the exposed men along the pike and the Southerners who held a momentary advantage of protection in the railroad cut. Yet reinforcements soon arrived from the other two regiments of Cutler's demi-brigade: the 84th and 95th New York further to Dawes's left. Dawes shouted to Major Edward Pye of the 95th, "We must charge!"

Davis's Confederates must have been exhausted at this point, having pushed forward that morning all the way from Cashtown. The 2nd Mississippi planted their colors near a low point in the railroad swale. The 42nd Mississippi was on their right and situated in a deeper portion of the cut. The 55th North Carolina was on the left, but an officer in the 2nd Mississippi wrote afterwards that men were jumbled together without organization. Rebel officers attempted to organize their own charge, but it proved to be too difficult and too late.

The three Northern regiments hurried across the open ground toward the railroad cut under a murderous fire. "Align on the colors!" Dawes commanded his men, "Close up on the colors!" The 6th Wisconsin's colors fell several times during the charge. Dawes later estimated that 420 of his men started from the road and only 240 reached the cut. There was a particular melee for the tempting colors of the 2nd Mississippi as several Yankees were shot down while trying to grab the prize. Rufus Dawes reached the embankment amid cries of "Throw down your muskets!" He

looked down four feet to find himself "face to face with hundreds of Rebels."

About twenty men from the 6th Wisconsin quickly positioned themselves along the eastern (and shallower) end of the cut to fire into it. The quick-thinking Dawes immediately called for the Confederate officer in command to step forward. "Surrender or I will fire!" The officer, later identified as Major John Blair of the 2nd Mississippi, surrendered his sword without a word. The men under his command took the queue and dropped their muskets. Recalling the events later, Dawes marveled at the discipline of his own men in withholding their fire. They saved hundreds of Southern lives in the "fearful excitement of the moment." Although in grim reality, there were also complaints of men continuing to fire after having "surrendered."

Many Confederates managed to scurry away and escape westbound toward Herr Ridge. Dawes estimated afterwards that he and his men bagged 232 prisoners. Whatever the actual number, General Joe Davis was not among those casualties. His whereabouts in the action have never been definitively ascertained. "I gave the order to retire," he reported simply, "which was done in good order, leaving some officers and men in the railroad cut, who were captured, although every effort was made to withdraw all the commands."

In the meantime, since the Army of the Potomac's Eleventh Corps had followed Reynolds's First Corps to Gettysburg, General Howard rode ahead while waiting for the arrival of his three divisions and artillery. Howard originally planned to encamp along the Emmitsburg Road south of town in the vicinity of fruit dealer Joseph Sherfy's peach orchard. Howard heard gunfire and saw the long line of First Corps troops ahead of him cutting

Profile:
Major General Oliver Howard (1830–1909)

▲ Major General Oliver Howard led the Eleventh Corps in the Army of the Potomac. Howard commanded the Gettysburg battlefield during the afternoon of July 1 after Reynolds's death. While his forces suffered defeat north and west of Gettysburg, he selected Cemetery Hill as a rallying point. (Library of Congress)

The "Christian General," Oliver Otis Howard was born in 1830, making him 32 years old and Meade's youngest corps commander at Gettysburg. The Maine native graduated from Bowdoin College in 1850 and West Point in 1854, ranking fourth in his class. In 1857, while campaigning in Florida against the Seminoles, the already religious officer underwent a conversion to evangelical Christianity. He remained in the army, and his newfound piety sometimes earned him ridicule from peers and those serving under him.

Howard commanded a brigade temporarily at First Bull Run and advanced to brigadier general effective September 1861. Commanding a brigade in the Second Corps in the spring of 1862, Howard lost his right arm at Seven Pines and later received a Medal of Honor for his valor. He returned quickly in time for Second Manassas. At Antietam, he replaced wounded division commander John Sedgwick, and retained division command until the end of the year.

After promotion to major general in the spring of 1863, Howard replaced the popular immigrant Franz Sigel as commander of the Eleventh Corps. Howard's attempts to instill military and moral discipline did not win much popularity with the troops. At Chancellorsville, his corps held the unprepared right flank against Jackson's flank attack. Many in the army, right or wrong, blamed Howard and his "flying Dutchmen" as scapegoats for the rout. Other officers commented on the fact that Howard was a "perfect gentleman" but questioned if he had "the snap" to manage the Germans. He did not yet inspire confidence. Between dissension internally and accusations within the army, the Eleventh Corps entered Gettysburg in crisis.

Howard commanded the field at Gettysburg during the afternoon of July 1. His Eleventh Corps was put to the test once again, resulting in more criticism against their performance. Howard selected Cemetery Hill as the crucial rallying point for the Union army, however, and afterwards received the thanks of Congress (along with Hooker and Meade, in that order) for defeating Lee at Gettysburg.

across country toward Seminary Ridge. A messenger arrived from Reynolds with instructions to come up to Gettysburg. Howard then sent a staff officer in search of Reynolds for additional instructions.

General Howard and another officer then made a brief reconnaissance of the area. They rode to a prominent hill south of the town and near the local Evergreen Cemetery. From there, Howard had an excellent view. Seeing the military benefits of this Cemetery Hill, Howard remarked, "This seems to be a good position." Howard then continued into the town, where a local youth named Daniel Skelly led him to an observatory on the roof of a building occupied by a large dry goods store. Howard and a staff officer climbed into this observatory and swept the countryside with field glasses.

While Howard studied the landscape, a sergeant rode up and shouted from street level, "General Reynolds is wounded, sir." Howard offered his condolences and continued to observe the fighting north and west of town. At perhaps 10:30 a.m., a staff officer returned and announced, "General Reynolds is dead, and you are the senior officer on the field."

Howard then sent messages to Major General Carl Schurz placing him in temporary command of the Eleventh Corps, to Dan Sickles in Emmitsburg requesting the Third Corps come forward, and to the senior Major General Henry Slocum whose Twelfth Corps was only about five miles away at Two Taverns. "God helping us," Howard stated to those around him, "we will stay here until the army comes." Howard then established his headquarters on Cemetery Hill. General Howard, like Reynolds before him, exhibited no intent to fall back toward Maryland. The battle had been joined, and he would wait for the Army of the Potomac to hasten to his aid.

As 12:00 p.m. approached, combatants on both sides regrouped to lick their wounds and await further orders. The opening action had seen the death of Reynolds, the capture of Archer, and the mauling of Archer, Davis, and Cutler's brigades, with countless losses at the lower levels. Neither commanding general was on the field yet. From their respective distances, Meade and Lee were mostly blind as to what was occurring at Gettysburg.

◄ The Fahnestock building on Baltimore Street in Gettysburg. General Howard was observing the battlefield from the rear portion of the roof when he learned of Reynolds's death. This photo was taken around July 9 when the U.S. Sanitary Commission utilized the building. (Library of Congress)

Orders of Battle

Army of the Potomac: Major General Joseph Hooker / Major General George Meade

First Corps: Major General John Reynolds / Major General Abner Doubleday / Major General John Newton

First Division: Brigadier General James Wadsworth

First Brigade: Brigadier General Solomon Meredith / Colonel William Robinson

19th Indiana; 24th Michigan; 2nd, 6th, 7th Wisconsin

Second Brigade: Brigadier General Lysander Cutler

7th Indiana; 76th, 84th, 95th, 147th New York; 56th Pennsylvania

Second Division: Brigadier General John Robinson

First Brigade: Brigadier General Gabriel Paul / Colonel Samuel Leonard / Colonel Adrian Root / Colonel Richard Coulter / Colonel Peter Lyler

13th Massachusetts; 16th Maine; 94th, 104th New York; 107th Pennsylvania

Second Brigade: Brigadier General Henry Baxter

12th Massachusetts; 83rd, 97th New York; 11th, 88th, 90th Pennsylvania

Third Division: Brigadier General Thomas Rowley / Major General Abner Doubleday

First Brigade: Colonel Chapman Biddle / Brigadier General Thomas Rowley / Colonel Chapman Biddle

80th New York; 121st, 142nd, 151st Pennsylvania

Second Brigade: Colonel Roy Stone / Colonel Langhorne Wister / Colonel Edmund Dana

143rd, 149th, 150th Pennsylvania

Third Brigade: Brigadier General George Stannard / Colonel Francis Randall

12th, 13th, 14th, 15th, 16th Vermont

Artillery Brigade: Colonel Charles Wainwright—guns: 28

2nd Maine Battery B; 5th Maine Battery E; 1st New York Battery L; 1st Pennsylvania Battery B; 4th US Battery B

Second Corps: Major General Winfield Hancock / Brigadier General John Gibbon

First Division: Brigadier General John Caldwell

First Brigade Colonel Edward Cross / Colonel H. Boyd McKeen

5th New Hampshire; 61st New York; 81st, 148th Pennsylvania

Second Brigade: Colonel Pennsylvania Patrick Kelly

28th Massachusetts; 63rd, 69th, 88th New York; 116th Pennsylvania

Third Brigade: Brigadier General Samuel Zook / Lieutenant Colonel John Fraser

52nd, 57th, 66th New York; 140th Pennsylvania

Fourth Brigade: Colonel John Brooke

27th Connecticut; 2nd Delaware; 64th New York; 53rd, 145th Pennsylvania

Second Division: Brigadier General John Gibbon / Brigadier General William Harrow

First Brigade: Brigadier General William Harrow / Colonel Francis Heath

15th Massachusetts; 19th Maine; 1st Minnesota; 82nd New York

Second Brigade: Brigadier General Alexander Webb

69th, 71st, 72nd, 106th Pennsylvania

Third Brigade: Colonel Norman Hall

19th, 20th Massachusetts; 7th Michigan; 42nd, 59th New York

Third Division: Brigadier General Alexander Hays

First Brigade: Colonel Samuel Carroll

14th Indiana; 4th, 8th Ohio; 7th West Virginia

Second Brigade: Colonel Thomas Smyth / Lieutenant Colonel Francis Pierce

14th Connecticut; 1st Delaware; 12th New Jersey; 10th, 108th New York

Third Brigade: Colonel George Willard / Colonel Eliakim Sherrill / Lieutenant Colonel James Bull

39th, 111th, 125th, 126th New York

Artillery Brigade: Captain John Hazard—guns: 28

1st New York Lieutenant Battery B; 14th New York Battery; 1st Rhode Island Battery A, Battery B; 1st US Battery I; 4th US Battery A

Third Corps: Major General Daniel Sickles / Major General David Birney

First Division: Major General David Birney / Brigadier General J. H. Hobart Ward

First Brigade: Brigadier General Charles Graham / Colonel Andrew Tippin
57th, 63rd, 68th, 105th, 114th, 141st Pennsylvania

Second Brigade: Brigadier General J. H. Hobart Ward / Colonel Hiram Berdan
20th Indiana; 3rd, 4th Maine; 86th, 124th New York; 99th Pennsylvania;
1st, 2nd US Sharpshooters

Third Brigade: Colonel Regis de Trobriand
17th Maine; 3rd, 5th Michigan; 40th New York; 110th Pennsylvania

Second Division: Brigadier General Andrew Humphreys

First Brigade: Brigadier General Joseph Carr
1st, 11th, 16th Massachusetts; 12th New Hampshire; 11th New Jersey; 26th Pennsylvania

Second Brigade: Colonel William Brewster
70th, 71st, 72nd, 73rd, 74th, 120th New York

Third Brigade: Colonel George Burling
2nd New Hampshire; 5th, 6th, 7th, 8th New Jersey; 115th Pennsylvania

Artillery Brigade: Captain George Randolph / Captain Judson Clark—guns: 30
1st New Jersey Battery B; 1st New York Battery D; 1st Rhode Island Battery E; 4th US Battery K; 4th New York Battery

Fifth Corps: Major General George Sykes

First Division: Brigadier General James Barnes

First Brigade: Colonel William Tilton
18th, 22nd Massachusetts; 1st Michigan; 118th Pennsylvania

Second Brigade: Colonel Jacob Sweitzer
9th, 32nd Massachusetts; 4th Michigan; 62nd Pennsylvania

Third Brigade: Colonel Strong Vincent / Colonel James Rice
20th Maine; 16th Michigan; 44th New York; 83rd Pennsylvania

Second Division: Romeyn Ayres

First Brigade: Colonel Hannibal Day
3rd, 4th, 6th, 12th, 14th US Regulars

Second Brigade: Colonel Sidney Burbank
2nd, 7th, 10th, 11th, 17th US Regulars

Third Brigade: Brigadier General Stephen Weed / Colonel Kenner Garrard
140th, 146th New York; 91st, 155th Pennsylvania

Third Division: Brigadier General Samuel Crawford

First Brigade: Colonel William McCandless
1st, 2nd, 6th, 13th Pennsylvania Reserves

Third Brigade: Colonel Joseph Fisher
5th, 9th, 10th, 11th, 12th Pennsylvania Reserves

Artillery Brigade: Captain Augustus Martin—guns: 26
5th US Battery D, Battery I; 1st Ohio Battery L; 3rd Massachusetts Battery C; 1st New York Battery C

Sixth Corps: Major General John Sedgwick

First Division: Brigadier General Horatio Wright

First Brigade: Brigadier General Alfred T. A. Torbert
1st, 2nd, 3rd, 4th, 15th New Jersey

Second Brigade: Brigadier General Joseph Bartlett
5th Maine; 121 New York; 95th, 96th Pennsylvania

Third Brigade: Brigadier General David Russell
6th Maine; 49th, 119th Pennsylvania; 5th Wisconsin

Second Division: Brigadier General Albion Howe

Second Brigade: Colonel Lewis Grant
2nd, 3rd, 4th, 5th, 6th Vermont

Third Brigade: Brigadier General Thomas Neill
7th Maine; 33rd, 43rd, 49th, 77th New York; 61st Pennsylvania

Third Division: Major General John Newton / Brigadier General Frank Wheaton

First Brigade: Brigadier General Alexander Shaler
65th, 67th, 122nd New York; 23rd, 82nd Pennsylvania

Second Brigade: Colonel Henry Eustis
7th, 10th, 37th Massachusetts; 2nd Rhode Island

Third Brigade: Brigadier General Frank Wheaton /
   Colonel David Nevin
      62nd New York; 93rd, 98th, 102nd, 139th
      Pennsylvania
Artillery Brigade: Colonel Charles Tompkins—guns: 48
   1st Massachusetts Battery A; 1st, 3rd New York;
      1st Rhode Island Battery C; 1st Rhode Island
      Battery G; 2nd US Battery D, Battery G; 5th US
      Battery F

Eleventh Corps: Major General Oliver Howard / Major General Carl Schurz

**First Division: Brigadier General Francis Barlow /
   Brigadier General Adelbert Ames**
   First Brigade: Colonel Leopold von Gilsa
      41st, 54th, 68th New York; 153rd Pennsylvania
   Second Brigade: Brigadier General Adelbert Ames /
      Colonel Andrew Harris
      17th Connecticut; 25th, 75th, 107th Ohio

**Second Division: Brigadier General Adolph von
   Steinwehr**
   First Brigade: Colonel Charles Coster
      134th, 154th New York; 27th, 73rd Pennsylvania
   Second Brigade: Colonel Orlando Smith
      33rd Massachusetts; 136th New York; 55th,
      73rd Ohio

**Third Division: Major General Carl Schurz / Brigadier
   General Alexander Schimmelfennig**
   First Brigade: Brigadier General Alexander
      Schimmelfennig / Colonel George von Amsberg
      82nd Illinois; 45th, 157th New York; 61st Ohio;
      74th Pennsylvania
   Second Brigade: Colonel Wladimir Krzyzanowski
      58th, 119th New York; 82nd Ohio; 75th
      Pennsylvania; 26th Wisconsin
Artillery Brigade: Major Thomas Osborn—guns: 26
   13th New York, 1st New York Battery I; 1st Ohio
      Battery I, 1st Ohio Battery K; 4th US Battery G

**Twelfth Corps: Major General Henry Slocum /
Brigadier General Alpheus Williams**

**First Division: Brigadier General Alpheus Williams /
   Brigadier General Thomas Ruger**
   First Brigade: Colonel Archibald McDougall
      5th, 20th Connecticut; 3rd Maryland; 123rd,
         145th New York; 46th Pennsylvania
   Second Brigade: Brigadier General Henry
      Lockwood
      1st Maryland Eastern Shore, 1st Maryland
         Potomac Home Brigade; 150th New York
   Third Brigade: Brigadier General Thomas H. Ruger /
      Colonel Silas Colgrove
      27th Indiana; 2nd Massachusetts; 13th New
         Jersey; 107th New York; 3rd Wisconsin

Second Division: Brigadier General John Geary
   1st Brigade: Colonel Charles Candy
      5th, 7th, 29th, 66th Ohio; 28th, 147th
      Pennsylvania
   Second Brigade: Colonel George Cobham /
      Brigadier General Thomas Kane
      29th, 109th, 111th Pennsylvania
   Third Brigade: Brigadier General George Greene
      60th, 78th, 102nd, 137th, 149th New York

Artillery Brigade: Lieutenant Edward Muhlenberg—
   guns: 20
   1st New York Battery M; 1st Pennsylvania
      Lieutenant Battery E; 4th US Battery F; 5th US
      Battery K

Artillery Reserve: Brigadier General Robert Tyler

First Regular Brigade: Captain Dunbar Ransom—
   guns: 24
   1st US Battery H; 3rd US Battery F, K; 4th US
      Battery C; 5th US Battery C

First Volunteer Brigade: Lieutenant Colonel Freeman
   McGilvery—guns: 22
   5th Massachusetts Battery E, 9th Massachusetts
      Battery; 15th New York; 1st Pennsylvania
      Battery C, F

Second Volunteer Brigade: Captain Elijah Taft—guns: 12
   2nd Connecticut Battery; 5th New York Battery

Third Volunteer Brigade: Captain James Huntington—guns: 20

1st New Hampshire Battery; 1st Ohio Battery H; 1st Pennsylvania Battery F, G; 1st West Virginia Battery C

Fourth Volunteer Brigade: Captain Robert Fitzhugh—guns: 24 guns

6th Maine Battery F; Maryland Battery A; 1st New Jersey Battery A; 1st New York Battery G, K

Cavalry Corps: Major General Alfred Pleasonton

First Division: Brigadier General John Buford

First Brigade: Colonel William Gamble

8th, 12th Illinois; 3rd Indiana; 8th New York

Second Brigade: Colonel Thomas Devin

6th, 9th New York; 17th Pennsylvania; 3rd West Virginia

Reserve Brigade: Brigadier General Wesley Merritt

6th Pennsylvania; 1st, 2nd, 5th, 6th US

Second Division: Brigadier General David Gregg

First Brigade: Colonel John McIntosh

1st Massachusetts; 1st Maryland, Purnell

Maryland Legion; 1st New Jersey; 1st, 3rd Pennsylvania

Second Brigade: Colonel Pennock Huey

2nd, 4th New York; 6th Ohio; 8th Pennsylvania

Third Brigade: Colonel J. Irwin Gregg

1st Maine; 10th New York; 4th, 16th Pennsylvania

Third Division: Brigadier General Judson Kilpatrick

1st Brigade: Brigadier General Elon Farnsworth / Colonel Nathaniel Richmond

5th New York; 18th Pennsylvania; 1st Vermont; 1st West Virginia

Second Brigade: Brigadier General George Custer

1st, 5th, 6th, 7th Michigan

Horse Artillery

First Brigade: Captain James Robertson—guns: 28

2nd US Battery B, L, M; 4th US Battery E; 6th New York Battery; 9th Michigan Battery

Second Brigade: Captain John Tidball—guns: 20

1st US Battery E, G, K; 2nd US Battery A

Army of Northern Virginia: General Robert E. Lee

First Corps: Lieutenant General James Longstreet

Hood's Division: Major General John Bell Hood / Brigadier General Evander Law

Law's Brigade: Brigadier General Evander Law / Colonel James Sheffield

4th, 15th, 44th, 47th, 48th Alabama

Robertson's Brigade: Brigadier General Jerome Robertson

1st, 4th, 5th Texas; 3rd Arkansas

Anderson's Brigade: Brigadier General George T. Anderson / Lieutenant Colonel William Luffman / Colonel W. W. White

7th, 8th, 9th, 11th, 59th Georgia

Benning's Brigade: Brigadier General Henry Benning

2nd, 15th, 17th, 20th Georgia

Henry's Artillery Battalion—Major Mathis Henry—guns: 19

Latham's, Bachman's, Garden's, and Reilly's Batteries

McLaws's Division: Major General Lafayette McLaws

Kershaw's Brigade: Brigadier General Joseph Kershaw

2nd, 3rd, 7th, 8th, 15th South Carolina; 3rd South Carolina Battalion

Semmes's Brigade: Brigadier General Paul Semmes / Colonel Goode Bryan

10th, 50th, 51st, 53rd Georgia

Barksdale's Brigade: Brigadier General William Barksdale / Colonel Benjamin Humphreys

13th, 17th, 18th, 21st Mississippi

Wofford's Brigade: Brigadier General William Wofford

16th, 18th, 24th Georgia, Cobb's Legion, Phillips's Legion, 3rd Georgia Battalion Sharpshooters

Cabell's Artillery Battalion: Colonel Henry Cabell—guns: 16

Manly's, Carlton's, Fraser's, McCarthy's Batteries

Pickett's Division: Major General George Pickett

Kemper's Brigade: Brigadier General James Kemper
/ Colonel Joseph Mayo
1st, 3rd, 7th, 11th, 24th Virginia

Garnett's Brigade: Brigadier General Richard
Garnett / Major Charles Payton
8th, 18th, 19th, 28th, 56th Virginia

Armistead's Brigade: Brigadier General Lewis
Armistead / Colonel William Aylett
9th, 14th, 38th, 53rd, 57th Virginia

Dearing's Artillery Battalion: Major James
Dearing—guns: 18
Stribling's, Caskie's, Macon's, Blount's Batteries

First Corps Artillery Reserve: Colonel James Walton /
Colonel E. Porter Alexander

Alexander's Battalion: Colonel E. Porter
Alexander—guns: 24
Moody's, Gilbert's, Woolfolk's, Jordan's, Parker's,
Taylor's Batteries

Eshleman's Battalion: Major Benjamin Eshleman—
guns: 10
Squires's, Richardson's, Miller's, Norcom's
Batteries

Second Corps: Lieutenant General Richard Ewell

Rodes's Division: Major General Robert Rodes

Doles's Brigade: Brigadier General George Doles
4th, 12th, 21st, 44th Georgia

Daniel's Brigade: Brigadier General Junius Daniel
32nd, 43rd, 45th, 53rd North Carolina, 2nd North
Carolina Battalion

Iverson's Brigade: Brigadier General Alfred Iverson
5th, 12th, 20th, 23rd North Carolina

Ramseur's Brigade: Brigadier General Stephen
Ramseur
2nd, 4th, 14th, 30th North Carolina

O'Neal's Brigade: Colonel Edward O'Neal
3rd, 5th, 6th, 12th, 26th Alabama

Carter's Artillery Battalion: Lieutenant Colonel
Thomas Carter—guns: 16
Reese's, W. Carter's, Page's, Fry's Batteries

Early's Division: Major General Jubal Early

Gordon's Brigade: Brigadier General John Gordon
13th, 26th, 31st, 38th, 60th, 61st Georgia

Hays's Brigade: Brigadier General Harry Hays
5th, 6th, 7th, 8th, 9th Louisiana

Hoke's Brigade: Colonel Isaac Avery / Colonel
Archibald Godwin
6th, 21st, 57th North Carolina

Smith's Brigade: Brigadier General William Smith
31st, 49th, 52nd Virginia

Jones's Artillery Battalion: Lieutenant Colonel Hilary
Jones—guns: 16
Carrington's, Tanner's, Green's, Garber's
Batteries

Johnson's Division: Major General Edward Johnson

Steuart's Brigade: Brigadier General George
Steuart
1st Maryland Battalion; 1st, 3rd North Carolina;
10th, 23rd, 37th Virginia

Nicholls's Brigade: Colonel Jesse Williams
1st, 2nd, 10th, 14th, 15th Louisiana

Walker's Brigade: Brigadier General James Walker
2nd, 4th, 5th, 27th, 33rd Virginia

Jones's Brigade: Brigadier General John Jones /
Lieutenant Colonel Richard Dungan
21st, 25th, 42nd, 44th, 48th, 50th Virginia

Snowden's Artillery Battalion: Major James Latimer
/ Captain Charles Raine—guns: 16
Dement's, Carpenter's, Brown's, Raine's Batteries

Second Corps Artillery Reserve: Colonel J. Thompson
Brown

Dance's Battalion: Captain Willis Dance—guns: 20
Watson's, Smith's, Cunningham's, Graham's,
Griffin's Batteries

Nelson's Battalion: Lieutenant Colonel William
Nelson—guns: 10
Kirkpatrick's, Milledge's, Massie's Batteries

Third Corps: Lieutenant General Ambrose Powell Hill

Heth's Division: Major General Henry Heth / Brigadier
General J. Johnston Pettigrew

Archer's Brigade: Brigadier General James Archer /
Colonel Birkett Fry / Lieutenant Colonel Samuel
Shepard
1st, 7th, 14th Tennessee; 13th Alabama, 5th
Alabama Battalion

Davis's Brigade: Brigadier General Joseph Davis
2nd, 11th, 42nd Mississippi; 55th North Carolina

Pettigrew's Brigade: Brigadier General J. Johnston
Pettigrew / Colonel James K. Marshall / Major
John Jones

11th, 26th, 47th, 52nd North Carolina

Brockenbrough's Brigade: Colonel John
Brockenbrough
40th, 47th, 55th Virginia; 22nd Virginia Battalion

Garnett's Artillery Battalion: Lieutenant Colonel
John Garnett—guns: 15
Maurin's, Moore's, Lewis's, Grandy's Batteries

Pender's Division: Major General W. Dorsey Pender

McGowan's Brigade: Colonel Abner Perrin
1st, 12th, 13th, 14th South Carolina; 1st South
Carolina Rifles

Lane's Brigade: Brigadier General James Lane /
Colonel Clark Avery
7th, 18th, 28th, 33rd, 37th North Carolina

Scales's Brigade: Brigadier General Alfred Scales
/ Lieutenant Colonel George Gordon / Colonel
William Lowrance
13th, 16th, 22nd, 34th, 38th North Carolina

Thomas's Brigade: Brigadier General Edward
Thomas
14th, 35th, 45th, 49th Georgia

Pogue's Artillery Battalion: Major William Pogue—
guns: 16
Wyatt's, Graham's, Ward's, Brooke's Batteries

Anderson's Division: Major General Richard Anderson

Wilcox's Brigade: Brigadier General Cadmus Wilcox
8th, 9th, 10th, 11th, 14th Alabama

Perry's Brigade: Colonel David Lang
2nd, 5th, 8th Florida

Wright's Brigade: Brigadier General Ambrose
Wright
3rd, 22nd, 48th Georgia; 2nd Georgia Battalion

Posey's Brigade: Brigadier General Carnot Posey
12th, 16th, 19th, 48th Mississippi

Mahone's Brigade: Brigadier General William
Mahone
6th, 12th, 16th, 41st, 61st Virginia

Lane's Artillery Battalion: Major John Lane—17 guns
Sumter artillery: Ross's, Paterson's, Wingfield's
batteries

Third Corps Artillery Reserve: Colonel R. Lindsay Walker

McIntosh's Battalion: Major David McIntosh—guns:
16
Rice's, Hurt's, Wallace's, Johnson's Batteries

Pegram's Battalion: Major William Pegram /
Captain Edward Brunson—guns: 20
Crenshaw's, Marye's, Brander's, Zimmerman's,
McGraw's Batteries

Cavalry Division: Major General J. E. B. Stuart

Hampton's Brigade: Brigadier General Wade
Hampton / Colonel Lawrence Baker
1st, 2nd South Carolina; 1st North Carolina;
Cobb's Georgia Legion Cavalry; Phillips's
Georgia Legion; Jeff Mississippi Davis's
Legion

Fitzhugh Lee's Brigade: Brigadier General Fitzhugh
Lee
1st, 2nd, 3rd, 4th, 5th Virginia; 1st Maryland
Battalion

W. H. F. Lee's Brigade: Colonel John Chambliss
9th, 10th, 13th Virginia; 2nd North Carolina

Jenkins's Brigade: Brigadier General Albert Jenkins /
Colonel M. J. Ferguson
14th, 16th, 17th Virginia; 34th, 36th Virginia
Battalion

Horse Artillery: Major Robert Beckham—guns: 15
Breathed's, Chew's, Griffin's, Hart's, McGregor's
Batteries

Imboden's Command: Brigadier General John Imboden
(Not present at Gettysburg July 1–3)

18th Virginia; 62nd Virginia Mounted Infantry; Virginia
Partisan Rangers; Staunton (Virginia) Horse
Artillery Battery

Robertson's Brigade: Brigadier General Beverly
Robertson (Not present at Gettysburg July 1–3)

4th, 5th North Carolina

Jones's Brigade: Brigadier General William "Grumble"
Jones (Not present at Gettysburg July 1–3)

6th, 7th, 11th, 12th Virginia; 35th Virginia Battalion

Avoid a General Engagement

After the morning's fighting, additional elements of both armies arrived at Gettysburg during the afternoon hours of July 1. General Lee continued to caution against a major engagement, while A. P. Hill's Third Corps fought west of Gettysburg and Richard Ewell's Second Corps converged from the north. The Army of the Potomac's Eleventh Corps also arrived to assist Abner Doubleday's First Corps.

After having led the Army of Northern Virginia into Pennsylvania, General Ewell was reportedly unhappy to have Lee cancel his planned advance into Harrisburg. Mapmaker Jedediah Hotchkiss noted on June 29 that Ewell was "quite testy and hard to please" after receiving the news. Nevertheless, by the evening of June 30, Ewell accompanied the division of Major General Robert Rodes to Heidlersburg about nine miles northeast of Gettysburg. Another division under Jubal Early was located only about three miles east of Rodes. The Second Corps's last division under Major General Edward Johnson was previously ordered westward toward Scotland, Pennsylvania, in the Chambersburg vicinity. While at Heidlersburg, Ewell reported receiving orders from Lee "to proceed to Cashtown or Gettysburg, as circumstances might dictate, and a note from General A. P. Hill, saying he was at Cashtown." Generals Ewell, Rodes, and Early met that evening in Heidlersburg to discuss the situation.

They were joined by Major General Isaac Trimble. The 61-year-old Trimble was a West Point graduate, former civil engineer, and railroad construction engineer who had performed well under Stonewall Jackson in 1862. Trimble received a serious leg wound at Second Manassas in August 1862, and he recovered slowly. Trimble lobbied for his own advancement and received promotion to major general along with division command in January 1863. Trimble's health prevented his return to the army, however, until he arrived unsolicited in June while Lee's army was in Maryland. According to Trimble's recollections written years later, he immediately urged Lee to assign a brigade to capture Baltimore. This would have involved using men from A. P. Hill's Third Corps, and General Hill reportedly declined the idea. General Lee then told Trimble to join Ewell and assist the latter in capturing Harrisburg. Once again, according to Trimble, he volunteered to take that city with one brigade, but Ewell's

Second Corps received orders to rejoin the army's main body before anything came of the endeavor.

According to Trimble's account, which is not free from errors, Ewell expressed uncertainty and some agitation during this Heidlersburg consultation on June 30. Lee's orders were "read over repeatedly and variously commented on," while Ewell commented, "in severe terms on its ambiguity with reference to Cashtown or Gettysburg as the objective point." General Ewell even purportedly exclaimed, "Why can't a commanding General have someone on his staff who can write an intelligible order?"

General Rodes's division was in motion shortly after sunrise on July 1 with Ewell and Trimble in tow. Rodes's march route originally took his men west toward Cashtown via Middletown (modern-day Biglerville). Jubal Early's division, meanwhile, would follow. Shortly before reaching Middletown, however, Ewell received notice from General Hill that he was advancing toward Gettysburg. As a result, Ewell turned the head of Rodes's column south directly toward Gettysburg. Ewell also ordered Early to proceed to the same place on the Heidlersburg Road. Whether through skill, luck, or a combination of both, Ewell had two divisions approaching Gettysburg from the north (Rodes) and northeast (Early) on two separate roads. These movements contrasted with the remainder of Lee's army which spent the day bottled up west of Gettysburg on one road, i.e., the Chambersburg Pike.

Generals Ewell and Rodes discerned the sounds of battle when they were about four miles distant from Gettysburg. Continuing in that direction, they encountered and pushed back some of Devin's cavalry videttes from Buford's division. Around

12:00 p.m., Rodes's division arrived near a high prominence known as Oak Hill. From Oak Hill, while facing south toward Gettysburg, Ewell would have seen much of the morning's battlefield, a plain that extended toward the town, the right flank of Doubleday's First Corps, and Hill's men reforming on Herr Ridge about one mile to Rodes's right front.

Ewell also received a message from Lee, "in case we found the enemy's force very large, he [Lee] did not want a general engagement brought on till the rest of the army came up." Nevertheless, despite Lee's desire to avoid a general engagement, Hill's men had "already been warmly engaged." Ewell observed enemy troops which he thought were "rapidly preparing to attack me, while fresh masses were moving into position in my front." Ewell realized,

▲ Major General Isaac Trimble rode north with Ewell while hoping for a command of his own. Trimble's post-war writings helped perpetuate the image of a timid and indecisive General Ewell. (Library of Congress)

"It was too late to avoid an engagement without abandoning the position already taken up," so he "determined to push the attack vigorously."

The "fresh masses" of enemy observed by Ewell were elements of Howard's Eleventh Corps and Brigadier General John Robinson's First Corps division arriving on the scene. Having learned from Doubleday that the First Corps right was "hard pressed," Howard intended for his First and Third divisions, along with a battery of artillery for each, to seize and hold Oak Hill on Doubleday's right. Howard then assigned his remaining division and three batteries of artillery to remain with him in reserve on Cemetery Hill. His decision to hold Cemetery Hill proved to be a substantial one.

John Reynolds's morning death continued to have implications on the Union army's command structure. Brigadier General Alexander Schimmelfennig now led Carl Schurz's division, since Schurz temporarily commanded the Eleventh Corps while Howard took charge of the field. Schurz

▶ Oak Hill in the distance from the left side of the Eleventh Corps line in the foreground. The Eternal Light Peace Memorial, dedicated in 1938, dominates the hill today. Some Confederate artillery fought from the slope above the McLean farm. (Author's photo)

61

and Schimmelfennig advanced through the town with a below-average-strength division of about 3,100 men and began deployment on the flat plain north of town. "Either the enemy was before us in small force," Schurz wrote, "and then we had to push him with all possible vigor, or he had the principal part of his army there, and then we had to establish ourselves in a position which would enable us to maintain ourselves until the arrival of re-enforcements."

Around 12:30 p.m., Howard received confirmation from General Buford that the enemy was massing north and northeast of town. Given this news—and the realization that Rodes's men already occupied Oak Hill on Doubleday's right—Howard instead ordered Schurz to halt, prevent his own right flank from being turned, and support the First Corps by pushing forward a thick line of skirmishers. Rather than positioning themselves as an extension of Doubleday's right, Schurz and Schimmelfennig instead deployed behind the right and rear of the First Corps at an approximate right angle.

Brigadier General Francis Barlow's First Division of the Eleventh Corps followed Schimmelfennig's men through town. General Howard met Barlow and accompanied the division up Washington Street. It is uncertain how much tactical detail they discussed, but this was Howard's opportunity to reconnoiter the developing situation personally. As they rode northward, shells fired from artillery on Oak Hill occasionally burst overhead.

Years later, Howard recalled one young woman who remained on her porch to wave her handkerchief at the passing Northern soldiers. "How heartily they cheered her!" A projectile crashed into the back balcony of James Foster's house at the corner of Washington and High streets.

Fortunately, Foster's adult daughter Catherine vacated the porch moments earlier to get to street level and watch the Eleventh Corps march through town.

General Doubleday took the opportunity to strengthen his own position while Howard's Eleventh Corps reached the battlefield. The Iron Brigade returned to the east side of Willoughby's Run and reformed in Herbst Woods, which Doubleday later called "the key of the position." Doubleday placed Robinson's Second Division in reserve for a brief period near the Lutheran Seminary building.

Brigadier General John Robinson was a veteran officer known for his reliability, temper, and luxurious beard. An observer once dubbed him "the hairiest general I ever saw." Doubleday ordered Robinson to send one brigade north along Oak

▲ The "hairiest man in the army," Brigadier General John Robinson had a long and distinguished military career, despite being expelled from West Point for disciplinary reasons. His First Corps division held Oak Ridge during the afternoon of July 1. After Gettysburg, he expressed disappointment to General Meade for his division not being singled out in Meade's report. (Library of Congress)

▲ Brigadier General Henry Baxter was 41 years old at Gettysburg. His brigade's fight against Iverson's North Carolinians resulted in one of the battle's most one-sided engagements. (Library of Congress)

▶ Robinson's division position on Oak Ridge circa 1898 looking north toward Oak Hill. Note the post-war observation tower in the background. This image shows the tower at its original height. The tower stands shorter today after the National Park Service reduced its size during the 1960s. (Gettysburg National Military Park)

but vulnerable to the north (or right) where Ewell and Rodes were massing. Robinson selected the 1,450-man brigade of Brigadier General Henry Baxter for the assignment. Baxter was a former storekeeper and miller from Michigan who suffered four serious wounds during the war, suggesting a man who did not shirk from action. Baxter's presence attempted to lessen the gap between the First Corps on Oak Ridge and the Eleventh Corps on the plain below. Meanwhile, Robinson's other brigade under Brigadier General Gabriel Paul received orders to entrench and build barricades on Seminary Ridge.

In retrospect, Doubleday wrote in his report, "it might seem, in view of the fact that we were finally forced to retreat, that this would have been a proper time to retire." To withdraw without orders, however, "might have inflicted lasting disgrace upon the corps, and as General Reynolds, who was high in the confidence of General Meade, had formed his lines to resist the entrance of the enemy into Gettysburg, I naturally supposed that it was the intention to defend the place." Doubleday noted particularly the junction

Ridge beyond the railroad cut to reinforce Cutler's brigade flank. Since being pushed back into the woods, Cutler's position was defensible potentially from the west,

of the road network at Gettysburg and the strategic significance which, in his opinion, would have been granted to Lee by its possession. Doubleday considered a retreat likely to demoralize his First Corps, dispirit the army, and encourage the enemy. Doubleday knew that Sickles and Slocum were "within striking distance" and that the Eleventh Corps was arriving with General Howard, who held seniority over Doubleday. "If circumstances required it, it was his [Howard's] place, not mine, to issue the [retreat] order."

With the benefit of hindsight, Howard might have been better served using this brief break in the action to pull the First and Eleventh Corps back, rather than committing more troops north of town. As it was, his small Eleventh Corps was deployed on low ground with no real connection to Doubleday's corps and enemy forces approaching from the north and northeast. While Howard's selection of Cemetery Hill as a reserve position proved decisive, he also withheld approximately one-third of his Eleventh Corps strength from the front line. The reason he likely committed, however, was due to a reasonable expectation that support from Slocum's Twelfth Corps and Sickles's Third Corps was imminent. Schurz and Doubleday's forces could presumably hold out until those two corps marched only a handful of miles to Gettysburg.

Throughout the day, George Meade remained headquartered at Taneytown, Maryland, approximately 12 miles south of Gettysburg. Major General Winfield Hancock of the Second Corps arrived at Taneytown around 11:00 a.m., pursuant to the prior day's marching orders. Meade explained his views to Hancock, but at this hour Meade was also uncertain of the situation at Gettysburg. According to Hancock, Meade "had made up his mind

to fight a battle on what was known as Pipe Creek" and "was then preparing an order for that movement." Although the time at which headquarters distributed Meade's Pipe Creek Circular is unclear, it was likely distributed by late morning or early afternoon. Regardless of the exact time, it was after Reynolds, Buford, and Doubleday already committed to Gettysburg.

Over the next 90 minutes, Meade received confirming messages that the enemy were advancing on Gettysburg and Reynolds was fighting (not withdrawing) before being subsequently killed. Meade initially considered the "possible failure of General Reynolds to receive the order to withdraw his command by the route through Taneytown," and intended to send Hancock's Second Corps to Gettysburg and help cover Reynolds's withdrawal. Upon learning of Reynolds's death, Meade instead directed Hancock after 1:00 p.m. to Gettysburg and "assume command of the corps there assembled … the Eleventh, First, and Third, at Emmitsburg. If you think the ground and position there a better one to fight a battle under existing circumstances, you will so advise the general, and he will order all the troops up." As Meade later acknowledged, not only was Hancock "fully aware" of Meade's intentions, but Gettysburg was "a place which I had never seen in my life." Meade needed an assessment to determine if it was a more advantageous position at which to concentrate the army.

As Hancock started for Gettysburg, there was the sticky matter of seniority to deal with. Despite Hancock's "superb" reputation as a hard-hitting old army officer, he was junior in seniority to every infantry corps commander except the Fifth Corps's George Sykes. Hancock reminded Meade that both Howard and Sickles were his seniors, but Meade assured Hancock

▲ The highly regarded Major General Winfield Hancock ranked low in seniority due to his promotion date as compared to the other corps commanders. General Meade selected Hancock to travel to Gettysburg and decide if it was a suitable place to concentrate the army. (Library of Congress)

Harmon farm. As was common practice at other residences and farms, the Harmons' male tenant farmer fled with their horses prior to the armies' arrival in hopes of protecting the valuable livestock. As a result, on July 1 the farm's only occupants were Rachel Harmon and her 16-year-old niece Amelia. The large Harmon property included a two-story colonial home from which the two women watched the morning's activities with great interest and anxiety. Amelia described "hundreds of galloping horses" and "the ominous boom of a cannon." A Minie ball crashed into a shutter near Rachel's head and an officer shouted, "Leave the window or you'll be killed!" Instead of seeking shelter in lower quarters, the women raced into their cupola where the landscape unfolded below them, "for everywhere had sprung up armed men, where but an hour ago only grass and flowers grew."

"The enemy had now been felt," Heth reported with some understatement, "and found to be in heavy force in and around Gettysburg." Heth reformed most of his division south of the Chambersburg Pike with Archer's remnants on the division's extreme right, Johnston Pettigrew's large brigade of about 2,600 men in the center, and Colonel John Brockenbrough's small brigade to Pettigrew's left. Joe Davis's survivors remained north of the pike as Heth acknowledged their "shattered condition" might best serve to "collect its stragglers." Behind (or west of) Heth's position, Major General Dorsey Pender brought up his large division of more than 6,600 men.

General Lee and his staff were riding eastbound near the summit of South Mountain that morning when they heard the ominous sounds of artillery fire in the distance. Lee's "Old War Horse" Longstreet rode with him for part of the way, but

that he had also received authority to appoint anyone as deemed "expedient." Hancock was not personally troubled by the matter but "knew that legally it was not proper, and that if they chose to resist it, it might become a very troublesome matter to me." (Perhaps because of this, Butterfield instructed Hancock that Henry Slocum would take command when he arrived on the field.) Hancock departed Taneytown for Gettysburg around 1:30 p.m. Since Meade was, at this hour, still unsure where the army would ultimately converge, Hancock was given the momentous latitude to determine if Gettysburg was the place to bring the army to.

While two of Richard Ewell's Confederate divisions converged on Gettysburg from the north, General Heth's battered division withdrew about one-half mile west of Willoughby's Run toward a woodlot beyond the sprawling Emanuel

Longstreet's First Corps was slowed and then halted by the arrival of the supply trains and wagons from Edward Johnson's division of the Second Corps having cut into the road in front of them. Lee's curiosity and anxiety was raised by the sounds of the gunfire and Lee rode faster toward the front along the troop-filled Chambersburg Pike.

Lee arrived next at A. P. Hill's headquarters in Cashtown. Hill's actions and presence on this day are a mystery. Some believe that he spent the morning sick in his cot, and only informed Lee that he knew "nothing" of activities in his front. It is likely Hill assumed his men had encountered the cavalry they expected to find. As Lee's staffer Walter Taylor wrote, "General Hill hastened to the front. General Lee followed." While near Cashtown, Ewell's staff officer Campbell Brown also arrived to notify Lee that Ewell had shifted his march destination from Cashtown to Gettysburg. Lee inquired if Ewell had received any word from J. E. B. Stuart and his anxiety over his missing cavalry arm was evident.

With their noontime arrival on Oak Hill, Richard Ewell and Robert Rodes realized they had received a great opportunity to strike the Union's First Corps's right flank on the hill's lower extension at Oak Ridge. "On arriving on the field," Rodes reported, "I found that by keeping along the wooded ridge … I could strike the force of the enemy with which General Hill's troops were engaged upon the flank, and that, besides moving under cover, whenever we struck the enemy we could engage him with the advantage in ground." Unfortunately, this took time to deploy and contributed to a pause in fighting of more than two hours.

Major General Robert Rodes looked the part of a general. The Virginia Military

Institute graduate was tall, blue eyed, and handsome. Historian Douglas Southall Freeman described Rodes as "a Norse God in Confederate gray." Rodes demonstrated his abilities as a brigade commander in several earlier battles and performed well again as a division commander under Jackson at Chancellorsville. Freeman's "Norse God," however, struggled at Gettysburg in charge of a large nearly 8,000-man division. Witnesses indicated that Rodes was noticeably ill with fever and riding in an ambulance when practicable. There was even speculation afterwards that some July 1 command challenges in the division might have resulted from the acquisition of an alcohol stash in Carlisle on June 28.

In front (south) of Oak Hill sat the prosperous farm of John and Mary Forney which bordered the Mummasburg Road.

▲ The 34-year-old Major General Robert Rodes was a VMI graduate and former assistant professor who fought in most major battles of the Eastern Theater. Rodes was considered to have great potential, but his division's attacks from Oak Hill were disjointed. (VMI Archives Photographs Collection, Virginia Military Institute Archives)

under Brigadier General Alfred Iverson formed near Forney's woods. To Iverson's left was the nearly 1,700-man Alabama brigade under Colonel Edward O'Neal. From right to left, the Alabamans extended down Oak Hill's eastern side, which slopes awkwardly and drops off more than 60 feet in front of the Moses McLean farm. These two brigades formed Rodes's front, but the terrain and the drop-off meant that Iverson's brigade would not be completely visible to most of O'Neal's men and vice versa.

To O'Neal's left as the plain flattened out toward the Carlisle Road, Major Eugene Blackford's sharpshooters from the 5th Alabama led the way. They were followed by Brigadier General George Doles's Georgia brigade of about 1,300 men. The 33-year-old Doles was highly regarded within the Army of Northern Virginia. A gap existed between Doles's right and O'Neal's left. Following behind were Brigadier General Junius Daniel's 2,100-man brigade, Lieutenant Colonel Thomas Carter's divisional artillery battalion, and Brigadier General Stephen Ramseur's

Fortunately, the Forneys vacated to the home of nearby relatives before armed combatants swarmed over their property. As Rodes's men reached Oak Hill, the nearly 1,400-man North Carolina brigade

▲ The Forney farm was prosperous in 1863, but it had become dilapidated by the time this image was taken in the 1930s. It was removed prior to the dedication of the Eternal Light Peace Memorial in 1938. Iverson's brigade attacked from the extreme right of the photo through to the left and passed the buildings. (Gettysburg National Military Park)

▼ Confederate artillery on the eastern slope of Oak Hill fired upon Eleventh Corps infantry and artillery positioned in the low ground north of Gettysburg. The open slope, however, also exposed the Southerners to return fire, despite their holding the advantage of the high ground. (Photo by Lynn Heller)

North Carolina brigade of roughly 1,000 men. Doles remained on the low plain, but Daniel, Carter, and Ramseur all filed off to their right and toward Oak Hill. Rodes ordered Daniel to form his large brigade about 200 yards behind Iverson's right. Ramseur's men were held in reserve for the time being.

Enjoying the advantage of a roughly 40-foot-tall elevation over Doubleday's right flank and a clear field of fire, Ewell, Rodes, and Lieutenant Colonel Carter assisted in posting the division's artillery of four 4-gun batteries on Oak Hill. Two batteries under captains William Carter and Charles Fry fronted south toward Chambersburg Pike. They were probably intended to supplement Hill's Third Corps artillery on Herr Ridge that threatened Doubleday from the west. Carter's two other batteries under captains Willam Reese and Richard Page soon unlimbered near Oak Hill's eastern slope and faced southeast. While enjoying the elevation, Oak Hill's slope toward the enemy also left these guns unconcealed and vulnerable. "The batteries fired with very decided effect," Lieutenant Colonel Carter reported, but he lamented the 11 casualties in Captain Carter's battery which resulted from their "exposed position" when the enemy returned fire.

Not only did Rodes's deployments consume time and allow their opponents opportunity to reorganize, but they also drew fire back to the Oak Hill position. Arriving with the Eleventh Corps in the plain north of town were six Napoleons from Battery I, 1st Ohio Light Artillery, under Captain Hubert Dilger. The 27-year-old Dilger was another German immigrant in the Eleventh Corps command chain and had relocated to Ohio at the beginning of the Civil War. Dilger distinguished himself at the battle of Chancellorsville and received a Medal of Honor in 1893 for that engagement. Dilger's battery unlimbered behind the brigade of Colonel George von Amsberg (replacing General Schimmelfennig, who led the division temporarily) and soon engaged in an artillery duel with Page and Reese's batteries near the eastern slope of Oak Hill. Approximately 30 minutes after Dilger opened fire, Lieutenant William Wheeler's 13th New York battery of four 3-inch rifles unlimbered on Dilger's right for additional support.

▼ Captain Hubert Dilger, a German artillery officer, commanded Battery I, First Ohio Light Artillery. Dilger's battery of six 12-pounder Napoleons supported the Eleventh Corps north of Gettysburg. Lieutenant William Wheeler's 13th New York Independent Battery unlimbered on Dilger's right. (Photo by Phil Spaugy)

Captain Page's battery suffered especially from this artillery exchange. General Rodes posted the guns initially in what has been described as sitting one above the other "like seats in an amphitheater." Lieutenant Colonel Carter, the artillery battalion commander, reported that Page was subjected to a "very destructive oblique fire" that created nearly 30 casualties along with 17 horses killed and disabled. When Carter assessed the damage, he confronted Rodes "mad as a hornet" and inquired, "General what fool put that battery yonder?" After an awkward pause, Rodes quietly replied, "You had better take it away Carter."

Near McPherson Ridge and the Chambersburg Pike, Federal batteries under Calef, Captain Gilbert Reynolds,

▼ Colonel Edward O'Neal was a 44-year-old Alabama native, as well as a former lawyer and judge. He had no military background and served as a colonel since 1862 while his potential promotion to brigadier general was held up. O'Neal served later as governor of Alabama from 1882 to 1886. (Alabama Department of Archives and History)

and James Cooper adjusted their positions and fronted north toward Oak Hill. Reynolds had been called upon to support Calef, but Carter's shells began to fall in among the battery while unlimbering. A piece of shrapnel or a stone struck Captain Reynolds below the eye and created a bloody wound. Eventually Calef's battery was ordered to rejoin Buford who had redeployed on the army's flanks, but Reynolds and Cooper likely exchanged fire with Rodes's men for nearly an hour.

Confusion soon took hold on Oak Hill. While the artillery exchanged fire, Rodes ordered General Iverson to halt his brigade and support a nearby battery, probably Captain William Carter's four guns. Rodes then told Iverson to advance gradually to support a battery that he intended placing in front of the infantry. Not understanding the expected timing of this last order, Iverson sent a staff officer to Rodes requesting clarification "and received instructions not to move until my skirmishers became hotly engaged." General Rodes, meanwhile, interpreted the First and Eleventh Corps's movements as being "directed upon the position which I held" and "being thus threatened from two directions, I determined to attack with my center and right."

"Finding that the enemy was rash enough to come out from the woods to attack me," Rodes continued, "I determined to meet him when he got to the foot of the hill I occupied, and, as he did so, I caused Iverson's brigade to advance, and at the same moment gave in person to O'Neal the order to attack, indicating to him precisely the point to which he was to direct the left of the four regiments then under his orders … Daniel was at the same moment instructed to advance to support Iverson, if necessary; if not, to attack on his right as soon as possible." The coordination Rodes intended for Iverson, O'Neal, and Daniel's attacks failed to materialize.

Colonel Edward O'Neal was a brigade commander who had not yet received promotion to brigadier general. Despite having been wounded several times and cited for past gallantry, Rodes harbored misgivings about the former lawyer and politician from Alabama. In preparing this assault, General Rodes detached the 5th Alabama from O'Neal to act as a reserve on the left under Rodes's immediate direction. This was an odd arrangement for a division commander who should have had bigger tasks at hand. Colonel O'Neal then complained that another of his regiments, the 3rd Alabama, received similar orders to connect with Daniel on the right. "Why my brigade was thus deprived of two regiments," O'Neal complained, "I have never been informed." General Rodes, on the other hand, blamed the 3rd Alabama's detachment on O'Neal.

Given such miscommunication, it is little wonder that Rodes acknowledged O'Neal's men "went into action in some confusion, and with only three of its regiments." The traditional interpretation is that O'Neal advanced before Iverson, although some historians debate that. What is clear is that both brigades advanced piecemeal and neither adequately supported the other. O'Neal's three remaining regiments advanced south toward the Mummasburg Road and against General Baxter's brigade, which had now taken position on Oak Ridge. Baxter's line was shaped like an inverted "V" with his right regiments facing north against O'Neal. Baxter also received assistance from Captain Francis Irsch and four companies of the 45th New York which advanced from the Eleventh Corps line toward the McLean farm and harassed O'Neal's left. To compound O'Neal's problems, Rodes discovered that the colonel had not advanced with his men as expected but was instead found

▼ Modern view of the Moses McLean barn looking east from Oak Hill. The McLean farm was leased to a tenant family in 1863. Beyond the barn is the plain that was occupied by the Eleventh Corps. Their monuments are visible in the middle distance. (Photo by Phil Spaugy)

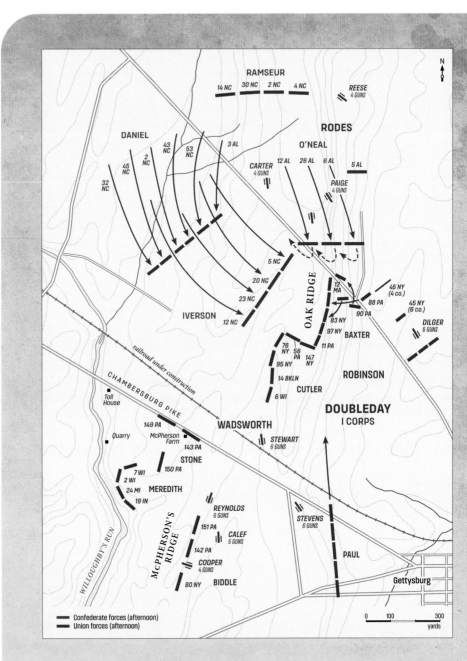

▲ Rodes's afternoon attack against Oak Ridge.

back with the 5th Alabama. As O'Neal noted in his report, "after a desperate and bloody fight of about half an hour, we were compelled to fall back."

According to General Iverson, he received orders from Rodes to "advance to meet the enemy, who were approaching to take the battery," and O'Neal's brigade "would advance on my left," while Daniel's brigade would support. As Iverson dispatched staff officers to notify his regiments and Daniel, he learned that O'Neal's men were already moving. It appears that Iverson had been uncertain of when to advance but pushed forward quickly when he learned that O'Neal was already in motion. In doing so, he apparently did not deploy skirmishers in front of his brigade.

Iverson's brigade comprised four North Carolina regiments (the 5th, 12th, 20th, and 23rd regiments) of slightly fewer than 1,400 men. Forming up on the northwest corner of the Forney farm, it was said afterwards that Iverson exhorted his men to "Give them hell!" With those words of encouragement,

Iverson promptly remained behind while his men moved forward unled, lacking skirmishers, and assuming O'Neal's cooperation on their left. Forney's rolling farm field was devoid of any cover as the Tar Heels tramped through fields of grass. The enemy's position was slightly more than 500 yards away and reached in only a handful of minutes.

Iverson's men moved in a southeasterly direction to strike the supposed right flank of the First Corps, which was obscured by woods, a low stone wall, and the reverse slope of Oak Ridge. "Along the path or eastern side of the field and on a ridge ran a stone fence which formed part of the enemy's line," wrote an officer of the 23rd North Carolina. "Behind this fence, alone, lay hidden from view, more men than our assaulting column contained." In advancing this way, the 5th North Carolina on the left of Iverson's brigade line pulled further away from the Mummasburg Road and dangerously exposed their left flank.

Private John Vautier of the 88th Pennsylvania described waiting for

▼ A modern view from the perspective of Iverson's men. The camera is near the farthest point of the Confederates' advance looking toward Oak Ridge. The battlefield monuments represent the positions of Baxter's brigade. The Northerners enjoyed concealment behind a wall that likely ran along the ridgetop's eastern side. One can see why Iverson's soldiers were largely oblivious to the Union strength that awaited them. (Author's photo)

Profile:
Brigadier General Alfred Iverson Jr. (1829–1911)

► Brigadier General Alfred Iverson is one of the most controversial officers who fought on July 1. His brigade suffered mass casualties assaulting Oak Ridge as allegations of incompetence, cowardice, and even drunkenness attached themselves to Iverson afterwards. (Gary Kross Collection)

Brigadier General Alfred Iverson Jr. was 34 years old at Gettysburg. The Georgia native was the son of a prominent United States congressman, senator, and secessionist. Young Iverson appeared to benefit throughout his career from his father's connections. Iverson's military career began during the Mexican War in a regiment raised by his father. He left the military in 1848 to practice law but returned in 1855 as a lieutenant in a cavalry regiment.

At the outset of the Civil War, Iverson received a commission as colonel of the 20th North Carolina Infantry from his father's friend, Confederate President Jefferson Davis. Iverson distinguished himself during the Seven Days and suffered a serious wound. He recovered and rejoined the Army of Northern Virginia for the 1862 Maryland campaign. The North Carolina brigade in which Iverson's regiment belonged broke after Brigadier General Samuel Garland's mortal wounding at South Mountain. Iverson's regiment also ran at Antietam, although he subsequently rallied them.

Afterwards, Iverson received promotion to brigadier general and replaced Garland as brigade commander. That is when the problems started.

Although Iverson had been promoted from one of the regiments in the brigade, North Carolinian officers, politicians, and newspapers openly complained about being led by an outsider from another state. The more senior Colonel Duncan McRae resigned in protest after being passed over. Governor Zebulon Vance publicly criticized the "mortifying" prospect of "entire brigades of North Carolina soldiers in the field commanded by strangers," as colonels from "distant states" received promotions over the heads of North Carolina's own officers. Newspapers called the practice "intolerable."

Unfortunately, General Iverson did little to win the respect or loyalty of his new command. His attempts to get a friend promoted as his replacement in his old regiment received protests from other officers. Iverson functioned as a strict disciplinarian, and yet some complained that any energy expended in organizing the brigade was more through the efforts of subordinates. At Chancellorsville, Iverson's brigade participated in Jackson's famous flank attack. Iverson raised eyebrows when he went to the rear personally to seek additional support, although he also received a wound from a spent shell. Accusations swirled that he was shirking. Already unpopular with his men, similar allegations of leading from behind would resurface against Iverson at Gettysburg.

Iverson's men on Oak Ridge. "The field in our front was swarming with Confederates who came sweeping on in a magnificent alignment, guns at right shoulder and colors to the front." After having likely already disposed of O'Neal's attack, most of Baxter's line shifted from facing O'Neal toward Forney's field, so as many as nine Federal regiments from both Cutler and Baxter's brigades waited in anticipation, with rifles cocked and fingers on their triggers.

When the North Carolinians were 80–100 yards from the wall, Baxter's men rose up and poured gunfire into them. Baxter's two right-most regiments, the 90th Pennsylvania and 12th Massachusetts, exploited Iverson's exposed left in a destructive left-oblique and enfilading fire. "A sheet of fire and smoke belched from the wall," wrote Private Vautier, "flashing full in the face of the Confederates. Hundreds of the Confederates fell at the first volley, plainly marking their line with the ghastly row of dead and wounded men, whose blood trailed the course of their line with a crimson stain clearly discernable for several days after the battle." One member of the 20th North Carolina recalled being hit four times, while five of the six comrades within his reach were killed.

Caught under fire in an open field, Iverson's beleaguered men enjoyed few options. Many went to ground immediately while others took refuge in a small, shallow gully a few hundred yards behind them. Captain Vines Turner of the 23rd North Carolina recalled being "unable to advance, unwilling to retreat, the brigade lay down in the hollow or depression in the field and fought as best it could." Dense smoke covered the field as the men vainly looked rearward for any assistance. Eventually many men surrendered and in the absence of white flags they hoisted

their hats or boots onto their bayonets as tokens of submission.

Where was General Iverson? Rumors swirled afterwards. One member of the 23rd North Carolina alleged that Iverson and his staff spent time hiding behind a log as he cautioned them not to look out more than one at a time. A member of Ramseur's rival brigade claimed Iverson was "drunk … and a coward besides" and "was off hiding somewhere." Iverson wrote in his report that he spent much of the time pleading with General Daniel to move forward in support and that he was promised a regiment would directly go to his men's assistance. It seems that Iverson led his brigade by trying to hurry support from the rear, as he had done at Chancellorsville. Iverson added his own observations to his post-battle report:

When I saw white handkerchiefs raised, and my line of battle still lying down in position, I characterized the surrender as disgraceful; but when I found afterward that 500 of my men were left lying dead and wounded on a line as straight as a dress parade, I exonerated, with one or two disgraceful individual exceptions, the survivors, and claim for the brigade that they nobly fought and died without a man running to the rear. No greater gallantry and heroism has been displayed during this war.

On the Federal side, General Baxter yelled, "Up boys and give them the steel!" Several of his regiments raced forward to bring in any willing prisoners. Many of Iverson's men could do little more than lie down to watch and wait for the Yankees to reach them. A member of the 12th Massachusetts recalled several hundred Rebels left their arms on the ground and ran to the Federal lines without much urging. Among the several First Corps monuments near Oak Ridge on

▲ The advance marker of the 88th Pennsylvania with the field of Iverson's attack in the background. This marker sits about 80 yards west of the Union position on Oak Ridge. The Pennsylvanians advanced approximately to this point and captured scores of prisoners. (Author's photo)

the battlefield in the present-day, a small advance marker for the 88th Pennsylvania commemorates the point about 80 yards from their stone wall defenses. Here they claimed credit for capturing two battle flags along with scores of Iverson's prisoners. The regiment's Sergeant Edward Gilligan earned a Medal of Honor for capturing the colors of the 23rd North Carolina. The color bearer would not give it up until Gilligan "reasoned with him with the butt of my rifle" and knocked the man down.

General Rodes reported that these "men fought and died like heroes." Unfortunately, their deaths were largely meaningless in the larger context of the battle. Modern estimates suggest the brigade suffered approximately 850 casualties (a 61% casualty rate) on July 1 alone, of which 176 were killed or mortally wounded and 674 wounded and / or captured. More dramatic was the description of a sickened young artillerist who saw the site the next day and observed, "Seventy-nine North Carolinians laying dead in a straight line. I stood on their right and looked down their line. It was perfectly dressed. Three had fallen to the front, the rest had fallen backward; yet the feet of all these dead men were in a perfectly straight line … They had evidently been killed by one volley of musketry."

Those of Iverson's men who fell on the field were buried in several shallow mass graves until the majority were exhumed and likely sent to Richmond in the summer of 1872. John Forney would show the killing field to visitors for years afterwards, as flattened or deformed bullets were still visible on the ground. It was said that as late as 1900 these "Iverson's Pits" were still plainly visible because the natural fertilizer made the surrounding grass or crops more luxuriant. Forney also warned visitors that the field held a "superstitious terror," and it proved difficult to keep laborers at work there as night approached.

General Rodes expected Junius Daniel's brigade to "advance to support Iverson, if necessary; if not, to attack on his right as soon as possible." Daniel was a North Carolina native and a West Point graduate. Daniel was detached from the Army of Northern Virginia during the winter of 1862/1863, but his was one of the brigades returned to Lee for the Pennsylvania campaign. Daniel enjoyed an excellent reputation for handling troops and combined it with an imposing physical presence. Yet, this was his first time leading his large 2,100-man brigade of five North Carolina regiments in an action of this magnitude.

◄ Brigadier General Junius Daniel's imposing physical presence was reportedly bolstered by his powerful voice that one man said could be heard a quarter of a mile away. His brigade made as many as three attempts against the Union positions on July 1 and suffered heavy losses in the process. (Warner, *Generals in Gray*, 67)

Daniel advanced behind Iverson but was unable to prevent the latter's destruction. Due to his position on the attacking right, Daniel was vulnerable not only to fire from Oak Ridge but also from Union troops along the Chambersburg Pike. As a result, Daniel split his brigade. Two regiments, the 43rd and 53rd North Carolina, headed toward Oak Ridge where they would presumably also connect with elements of O'Neal and Iverson's commands. Daniel's remaining regiments, the 2nd North Carolina Battalion and 45th North Carolina, advanced toward the pike while the 32nd North Carolina lagged further behind on their right.

The Federal First Corps troops along the Chambersburg Pike belonged to the brigade under Colonel Roy Stone. This brigade consisted of about 1,300 men in three Pennsylvania regiments—the 143rd, 149th, and 150th Pennsylvania Regiments. Colonel Stone served previously as major in the 13th Pennsylvania Reserves (also designated the 42nd Pennsylvania Infantry Regiment). The 13th Pennsylvania Reserves were nicknamed the "Bucktails" because the men of the regiment were considered superior marksmen, and each

soldier attached the tail of a deer he had shot to his cap. The regiment distinguished themselves such that Stone received orders in the summer of 1862 to recruit more Bucktails. Stone raised the 149th Pennsylvania and he received promotion as their colonel. Two more regiments were added to form a brigade, and Stone led this new brigade by the summer of 1863. Like their predecessors, Stone's new command also attached bucktails onto their forage caps and called themselves the "Bucktail Brigade." This angered the original Bucktails in the 13th Reserves, and they dubbed these newcomers the "Bogus Bucktails." Stone's newcomers lacked experience prior to Gettysburg, but the colonel was anxious to prove the value of his new Bucktails.

Colonel Stone's brigade formed on the right of the Iron Brigade near Herbst Woods. Stone faced potential threats from the north and west, while also closing a gap between the woods (which Doubleday intended to defend) and the Chambersburg Pike. They also received enfilade artillery fire from Confederate batteries on Herr Ridge. Stone ordered the 149th's colors to advance into the field about 50 yards

▶ After serving as a major in the 13th Pennsylvania Reserves, which was also known as the "Bucktails," Roy Stone recruited 20 companies of new Bucktails. Colonel Stone led this new brigade of three regiments at Gettysburg and defended the ground near the McPherson farm. Stone received a serious wound but survived. (U.S. Army Heritage and Education Center)

north of the Chambersburg Pike as a decoy to divert the enemy's shells. Color Sergeant Henry Brehm and five other men advanced and planted the colors on a pile of fence rails. The deception worked. The flag was visible above the surrounding wheat and continued to draw fire while the regiment's actual position was hidden from the Confederate artillerists.

As several of Daniel's regiments approached, Stone ordered the 149th Pennsylvania to the north side of the Chambersburg Pike toward the railroad

cut that witnessed fighting earlier that morning. Daniel's North Carolinians were within perhaps 30 yards of the cut when Stone's Bucktails opened fire and drove the Southerners back in confusion. Daniel's men soon reformed, attacked, and were repulsed again. Colonel Stone received a hip wound but remained on the field before turning command over to Colonel Langhorne Wister of the 150th Pennsylvania.

General Lee, meanwhile, arrived on the field at approximately 2:30 p.m. as Ewell's afternoon attacks were getting underway. Lee viewed the field from A. P. Hill's front, likely along or near the elevation of Herr Ridge. Lee confirmed the obvious at this point. The enemy was already present in considerable force and a general engagement could not be avoided. General Heth reported that after resting briefly following the morning's action, he received orders for his division to attack again with Dorsey Pender's division in support. As Ewell had taken position at a right angle on Hill's left, the Confederates again pressed forward in what Lee described as a "general advance" by both corps.

▶ This barn is the only remaining structure on the Edward McPherson farm, which witnessed heavy fighting on July 1. McPherson was a former member of the U.S. House of Representatives among other occupations, and like many battlefield landowners, he rented his property to tenant farmers. The barn and house served as a hospital afterwards. (Photo by Phil Spaugy)

The Whole Division Falling Back

In the afternoon, Robert E. Lee ordered a general advance of his forces against the Union army's position. The Army of the Potomac's Eleventh Corps defended weak ground north of Gettysburg and was eventually outflanked. The First Corps, which held McPherson Ridge for most of the day, received renewed attacks from A. P. Hill's men.

While Rodes's division was bungling the initial attacks against Oak Ridge, temporary Eleventh Corps commander Carl Schurz also struggled with his deployments in the open plain north of Gettysburg.

Carl Schurz was a well-educated German immigrant who arrived in America in 1852 after participating in a failed revolution. An anti-slavery advocate, Schurz supported Lincoln in the 1860 election as a prominent member of the new Republican Party and caught the president's attention. Schurz convinced Lincoln to grant him a commission as a brigadier general in 1862. His prominence encouraged political support for the war among German Americans, although his 1863 advancement to major general and division command angered more-experienced officers in the army. Schurz's division participated in the Chancellorsville debacle, and he vigorously defended his men against anti-immigrant criticism.

Schurz intended for his Third Division, which was commanded that day by Brigadier General Alexander Schimmelfennig, "to deploy on the right of the First Corps in two lines." Ideally, the Eleventh Corps would have extended the First Corps right to Oak Hill, but Rodes's division occupied the high ground there first. Schurz then received an order from Howard to push Schimmelfennig's skirmishers as far forward as possible. This

◀ Major General Carl Schurz was a German immigrant who arrived in America after participating in a failed revolution. An anti-slavery advocate and member of the new Republican Party, Schurz convinced Lincoln to grant him a commission. Schurz exercised field command of the Eleventh Corps on July 1 while Howard replaced Reynolds as wing commander. (Library of Congress)

▶ Brigadier General Alexander Schimmelfennig was a Prussian soldier and political revolutionary who immigrated into the United States. He served under fellow expatriate Carl Schurz, and temporarily commanded Schurz's division while the latter led the Eleventh Corps. (Ezra J. Warner, *Generals in Blue: Lives of the Union Commanders* [Baton Rouge, LA, 2013], 423)

was accomplished by four companies of the 45th New York, along with the 61st Ohio and 74th Pennsylvania. Their skirmish line stretched from the Mummasburg Road on the left to the Carlisle Road on the right.

Colonel Wladimir (or Włodzimierz) Krzyzanowski led the Second Brigade in Schimmelfennig's division. Krzyzanowski was a Polish noble who fled his home country after a failed 1846 uprising against Prussia. He enlisted in the Union army at the outbreak of the Civil War and became colonel of the 58th New York. President Lincoln appointed Krzyzanowski to brigadier general in November 1862, but the appointment expired when the Senate failed to confirm the promotion. A joke held that the expiration occurred because no one in Congress could pronounce Krzyzanowski's name. The brigade was among those outflanked and forced to retreat at Chancellorsville, and the men undoubtedly looked for redemption.

Krzyzanowski's brigade followed Colonel von Amsberg's brigade to the field. His regiments halted in the fields between the Mummasburg and Carlisle Roads just north of Pennsylvania College. While there, they were vulnerable to enemy artillery fire. Krzyzanowski's men suffered hits from Confederate overshots fired at Dilger's battery while waiting to go into action.

Next to arrive was Brigadier General Francis Barlow's First Division of the Eleventh Corps. Having fewer than 2,500 men, Barlow's division was the smallest in the Army of the Potomac. Upon their arrival, Schurz ordered Barlow's First

▶ Colonel Wladimir Krzyzanowski led the Second Brigade in Schurz's / Schimmelfennig's division. Krzyzanowski was another Eleventh Corps officer who had fled his homeland after a failed uprising. Krzyzanowski's brigade was among those forced to retreat at Chancellorsville, and his men undoubtedly hoped for battlefield redemption. (Library of Congress)

Brigade under Colonel Leopold von Gilsa to connect with Schimmelfennig's right. Brigadier General Adelbert Ames's Second Brigade, also of Barlow's division, was then directed to form in von Gilsa's right rear. Ideally, Barlow would protect Schimmelfennig's right flank, but the intended deployment did not remain in position for long.

In Barlow's front stood the buildings of the Adams County Almshouse, which had been established to care for the county's poor. Beyond the almshouse, a large knoll on the David Blocher property blocked a view of any enemy approach along the Harrisburg Road. This knoll also would have appeared to dominate Barlow's lower position, should the hill be occupied by enemy troops. Rock Creek was situated on the opposite (northeast) side of Blocher's Knoll. Further down the Harrisburg Road, Colonel Thomas Devin's cavalry pickets confirmed the approach of another body of enemy troops. This proved to be Jubal Early's division finally arriving from northeast of Gettysburg. General Doles's Georgians were also present to Barlow's left front near the Carlisle Road.

◄ This monument to the 74th Pennsylvania Volunteer Infantry Regiment is one of several memorials that today represent Schurz's Eleventh Corps battle line on modern Howard Avenue. The 74th Pennsylvania was part of General Schimmelfennig's brigade, which was temporarily commanded by Colonel George von Amsberg on July 1. The 334-man regiment suffered 33% casualties during the battle. (Author's photo)

Profile:
Brigadier General Francis Barlow (1834–96)

▲ Brigadier General Francis Barlow was ordered by General Schurz to defend the right flank of the Eleventh Corps. Barlow elected to extend his division to a small knoll in his front, which led to disastrous results when the Confederates attacked. (Library of Congress)

Francis Barlow did not look like your typical Civil War general. Barlow was clean-shaven, boyish, and frail looking, with a thin voice. A staff officer once observed that he appeared more like a newsboy. The 28-year-old minister's son graduated from Harvard and was practicing law in New York City when the Civil War started. In April 1861, he enlisted as a private in a New York regiment, and said a temporary goodbye to his new bride Arabella after only one day of marriage.

Barlow became a colonel by spring 1862 and distinguished himself at the regimental level. He received promotion to brigadier general after Antietam. His Eleventh Corps brigade was not in position to be steamrolled by Jackson at Chancellorsville and thus he avoided the shame that attached to much of the rest of the corps. General Howard promoted Barlow to division command after the defeat in the hopes that he would improve their performance. Barlow noted that his new command "is in a most disgusting condition as to discipline and morale. But if hard knocks and a tight rein will make them fight they will have to do it." Barlow was also not enamored with leading a large immigrant population and promised to "arrest them all the way down until I find some private soldier who will make them do things properly." Not surprisingly, his men viewed him as a taskmaster and Francis Barlow was not popular. Still, despite these question marks surrounding the general and his division, Barlow demonstrated a good track record at lower levels when he arrived on the field during the early afternoon of July 1. His liberal interpretation of his orders, however, resulted in one of the day's most controversial actions.

With no orders to do so from General Schurz, Barlow moved his division forward to the higher ground of Blocher's Knoll. Colonel von Gilsa's small brigade advanced first. The 68th New York, the 153rd Pennsylvania, and the 54th New York posted close to the top of the hill with a skirmish line in front along Rock Creek. The Yankees cleared some Confederate skirmishers from the knoll, perhaps confirming fears about the enemy occupying this high ground.

The 153rd Pennsylvania's nine-month enlistments had recently expired. Major John Frueauff met with the men and explained that while there was no disgrace

▲ A modern image looking from the former site of the Adams County Almshouse toward Blocher's Knoll (AKA Barlow's Knoll). This approximates the view General Barlow would have had on July 1. Note that the knoll blocks the sightlines of what lies beyond and potentially dominates Barlow's original position. (Author's photo)

◄ An engraving of 19-year-old Lieutenant Bayard Wilkeson commanding his battery on Blocher's (or Barlow's) Knoll. (Henry Hunt, "The First Day at Gettysburg," in *Battles and Leaders of the Civil War* [New York, 1887], 3: 280)

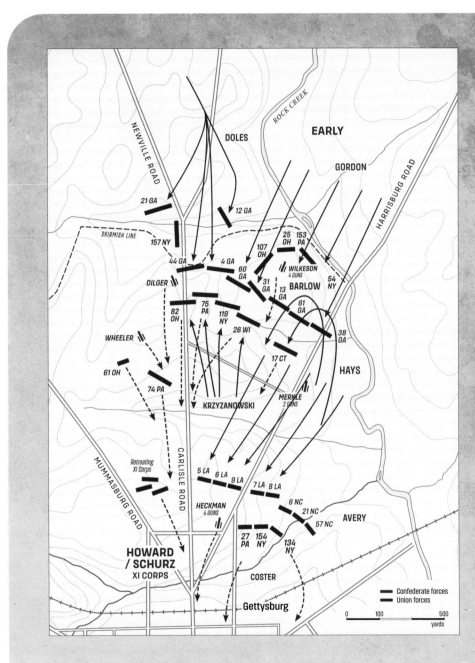

▲ Afternoon attacks by Early's division against Barlow and Coster.

in stepping out, "the enemy were in our native state, and that the people of Pennsylvania looked to us for relief, and that it was our duty to protect our homes." The men of the 153rd gave three cheers and not a man stepped out of ranks as they moved to Blocher's Knoll.

General Barlow received artillery support from 19-year-old Lieutenant Bayard Wilkeson's Battery G, 4th United States Artillery. Young Wilkeson was the son of war correspondent Samuel Wilkeson who was attached to the army. Two of Wilkeson's sections (four Napoleons) unlimbered near the summit while another section initially deployed in lower ground across the Harrisburg Road. Finally, Ames's brigade also moved to the knoll in support of Wilkeson. Four companies of the 17th Connecticut then deployed to secure the bridge over Rock Creek and the Josiah Benner property on the other side. Barlow's pieces were in their new positions by approximately 3:00 p.m.

While there were benefits from occupying the knoll, particularly observation and open fields of fire, Barlow's small division was now overextended. They were facing in two directions—northwest toward Doles's advancing brigade and northeast toward Early—and created a salient that was vulnerable to attack from two sides, while their own firepower was diffused in two directions. Barlow's flanks were in the air and his left had lost connection with Schimmelfennig's right. Finally, Barlow's advance occurred without the knowledge or permission of General Schurz, who was as surprised as anyone on the field when he observed it after the fact.

As Schurz had not ordered Barlow to occupy a specific piece of real estate, Schurz's biggest concerns were the disconnect between Barlow's new left and Schimmelfennig's right, along with

▲ Major General Jubal Early was Lee's "Bad Old Man" within the Army of Northern Virginia. Early's division arrived on the battlefield at an opportune time and played a decisive role in the Eleventh Corps's collapse. (Library of Congress)

the fact that Ames's brigade was no longer in echelon (behind the right rear). To remediate the first concern, Schurz "immediately gave orders to re-establish the connection" by advancing Krzyzanowski's brigade onto Barlow's new left. Facing north, Krzyzanowski's men strengthened the front against Doles's brigade but could not also help Barlow's right. Schurz only had so many men available to plug the increasing number of holes. He noted in his report that he "hurried off aide after aide" to General Howard on Cemetery Hill requesting a brigade from von Steinwehr's division, which Howard continued to hold in reserve.

Like the rest of Richard Ewell's Second Corps, Jubal Early's men started the day expecting to go to Cashtown. While on the march, Early received notification from Ewell that A. P. Hill and Robert Rodes

▲ Jones Avenue is one of the least visited sites in Gettysburg National Military Park. Lieutenant Colonel Hilary Jones's artillery battalion fired upon Barlow's advanced position from this open hill. Today it is a small strip of land surrounded by residential development. (Author's photo)

were moving toward Gettysburg and Ewell redirected Early there. As Early arrived in sight of Gettysburg, he discovered Rodes's division was already engaged to Early's right front. For the second time that afternoon, one of Ewell's divisions arrived fortuitously to strike a Federal flank.

Major General Jubal Early was described as abrasive, profane, and irascible. Balding and with an untrimmed beard, he was often stooped with rheumatism and appeared older than his 46 years. Early graduated from West Point in 1837, where his most memorable achievement was the moment future Confederate General Lewis Armistead allegedly broke a plate over his head.

A lawyer and politician prior to the Civil War, the Virginia native made brigadier general after impressing at First Bull Run. He went on to serve in almost every major Eastern Theater engagement. He received promotion to major general in spring 1863 and acted semi-independently at Second Fredericksburg during the Chancellorsville campaign.

He was reportedly the only officer permitted to swear in General Lee's presence, who referred to Early as "my bad old man." Southern historian Douglas Southall Freeman might have summarized Early's character best: "Unmarried, snarling and stooped, respected as a soldier but never widely popular as a man." The potential existed for conflict between Ewell's quirky but agreeable personality and the subordinate Early's quirky but bad-tempered and dominating persona.

The aggressive General Early formed his division for action astride the Harrisburg Road and only about 1,400 yards from Barlow's Knoll. The division's artillery unlimbered on a small elevation on the southeast side of the road. Lieutenant Colonel Hillary Jones positioned three batteries of 12 guns, while another battery was held in reserve. According to Jones, his guns "opened fire with considerable effect on the enemy's artillery, and upon the flank of a column of troops that were being massed upon our right."

Unfortunately, young Lieutenant Wilkeson's outgunned battery on Barlow's Knoll received this well-directed fire and suffered heavily. Wilkeson was badly exposed with no cover on the top of an open hill. The lieutenant remained mounted to supervise and steady his men. Within only a few short minutes of opening, a solid shot from one of Jones's pieces ripped into Wilkeson's horse, killing the poor animal and mangling Wilkeson's right leg.

Several of Wilkeson's men carried him off the field and to the nearby almshouse. With no medical treatment available, it is believed that the boy-lieutenant slowed the bleeding by using his pocketknife to tighten a tourniquet on his remaining stump. The story spread afterward that Wilkeson used his own knife to self-amputate his leg, but this might be apocryphal. Yet, he suffered in agony with no medical attention for several hours along with other wounded men in a dirty basement of the almshouse before dying. His journalist father arrived later and penned a July 4 dispatch from the battlefield that observed, "Who can write the history of a battle whose eyes are immovably fastened upon … the dead body of an oldest born, crushed by a shell in a position where a battery should never have been sent, and abandoned to death in a building where surgeons dared not to stay?"

Early's infantry then attacked. Leading the way were five Georgian regiments of about 1,500 men under Brigadier General John B. Gordon. (A sixth regiment, the 26th Georgia, was detached to support artillery.) Gordon was yet another attorney turned hard-hitting, aggressive Southern general. He had been wounded several times at Antietam including by a ball that passed through the left side of his face and left him disfigured. Nevertheless, one soldier considered him "the most prettiest thing you ever did see on a field of fight. It 'ud put fight into a whipped chicken just to look at him."

As Gordon's men advanced, the first opposition would have been the detachment from the 17th Connecticut posted at the Benner farm. The Nutmegger regiment under Major Allen Brady were already receiving artillery fire from Jones's battalion, and one round set the Benner house on fire. Both sides exchanged gunfire as Gordon approached and Brady's four companies eventually withdrew in the face of the superior numbers.

▲ Brigadier General John B. Gordon was a fiery Georgia native commanding a brigade in Jubal Early's division. Gordon's men spearheaded the attack against Barlow's position. (Library of Congress)

▲ Monuments sit atop Barlow's Knoll within today's Gettysburg National Military Park. This view is from the Confederate perspective along the Harrisburg Road. General Gordon's brigade attacked through the foreground and up the hill. (Author's photo)

▼ Brigadier General Adelbert Ames was a former sailor who started the war as an artillerist. Ames moved to the infantry branch to receive better promotional opportunities and became the original commander of the 20th Maine Regiment. Ames led a brigade under Francis Barlow at Gettysburg and took a poor position on Blocher's Knoll. (Library of Congress)

Gordon's pace quickened when about 300 yards from Colonel von Gilsa's line. Gordon described his brigade moving while under a heavy fire over fences and crossing Rock Creek, said to be two to three feet deep, as they "rushed upon the enemy with a resolution and spirit, in my opinion, rarely excelled." A soldier in the 61st Georgia observed afterwards, "we met the enemy at Rock Creek. We attacked them immediately, but we had a hard time moving them. We advanced with our accustomed yell, but they stood firm until we got near them."

Both sides traded volleys at only 75 yards distance, and the Northerners broke first. Not only were von Gilsa's two thin lines overextended and outnumbered, but they also glimpsed Brigadier General Harry Hays's brigade of 1,300 "Louisiana Tigers" following Gordon. Hays's men extended to the other side of the Harrisburg Road beyond Barlow's right flank. The common soldier in Gordon's 61st Georgia recalled the Yankees "began to retreat in fine order, shooting at us as they retreated. They were harder to drive than we had ever known them before. Men were being mowed down in great numbers on both sides."

General Barlow saw his men's fighting differently, as he wrote to his mother only a few days afterwards. "A force came up against our front in line of battle with supports in the rear. We ought to have held the place easily, for I had my entire force at the very point where the attack was made. But the enemies' skirmishers had hardly attacked us before my men began to run. No fight at all was made."

Confusion took hold as von Gilsa's retreating men crowded into General Ames's lines. Adelbert Ames was among the younger generals in the field, at only 28 years old, but he packed some experience into those years. He graduated 5th in his 1861 West Point class and fought as an artillerist at First Bull Run, for which he later received a Medal of Honor. He transferred to the infantry in the summer of 1862 as colonel of the 20th Maine. Like most West Point graduates, Ames was considered a disciplinarian and the 20th's Tom Chamberlain complained that the men might shoot the young colonel in their first battle. Nevertheless, Ames earned the men's respect and his coolness under fire reportedly inspired his Lieutenant Colonel Joshua Chamberlain. Ames received promotion to brigadier general after Chancellorsville (elevating Joshua Chamberlain to command of the 20th Maine), as fellow Maine-native Oliver Howard brought both Ames and Barlow to the Eleventh Corps to strengthen their discipline and capabilities.

Despite Ames's experience and bravery, his regimental dispositions on Blocher's Knoll were inadequate. As Wilkeson's battery started to retire, the 25th Ohio moved on von Gilsa's left and the 107th Ohio then formed on their left facing northwest, so the two regiments formed at a right angle. The 75th Ohio regiment and the six remaining companies of the 17th Connecticut then formed behind them. Ames's contribution to Barlow's line was

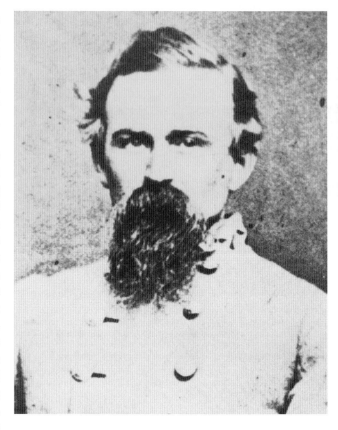

shaped something like a half-circle facing in two directions with exposed flanks.

On Barlow's right, von Gilsa's retreating men broke through the ranks of the 17th Connecticut. One soldier complained a "German regt. came running back, hooting & hollowing, right through our lines which broke our regt. all up & scattered us." Lieutenant Colonel Douglas Fowler, commander of the 17th Connecticut, ordered his men forward. "Charge bayonets!" Fowler remained mounted and ignored earlier pleas to dismount, as he feared such an act might be considered cowardly. Unfortunately, a bullet or shell fragment struck Fowler in the head and splattered his brains on a nearby adjutant.

General Doles's advancing Georgians pressed against Ames's left. The 107th Ohio received enfilading fire from

▲ Brigadier General George Doles was a successful businessman from Milledgeville, Georgia. His brigade crashed into the Eleventh Corps position near Carlisle Road. (Warner, *Generals in Gray*, 74)

The Barlow–Gordon Incident

After the war, General Gordon promoted a more romantic version of the Barlow wounding incident. In Gordon's recollections, which he gave in speeches and his memoirs, it was he who encountered Barlow on the field and attended to the wounded Northerner. Barlow requested, as "great tears came like a fountain and rolled down his pale face," for Gordon to destroy some letters of a personal nature from Mrs. Barlow that were in General Barlow's pocket. It was Gordon who then supervised Barlow's placement into the shade.

Gordon added another dramatic element to the story. Allegedly the two men were unknowingly seated next to each other at a dinner party years later. "General, are you related to the Barlow who was killed at Gettysburg?" "Why, I am the man sir. Are you related to the Gordon who killed me?" "I am the man, sir." Despite some inconsistencies, Barlow (who died in 1896) is not known to have ever confirmed or denied the story in his lifetime, leading some to cling to the notion that parts of the Barlow–Gordon story might be true. Or it might be another Gettysburg myth, encouraging those who want to cherish stories of enemies becoming friends on the field and in the long twilight afterwards.

Doles's regiments, while the 25th Ohio received the same from Gordon's men. General Ames ordered his 75th Ohio to fix bayonets in a vain attempt to check the enemy. "It was a fearful advance and made at a dreadful cost of life," recalled Colonel Andrew Harris of the 75th. "We could go no farther, halted and opened fire. We checked them in our immediate front, but they continued to press on around both flanks." Colonel Harris expected additional assistance or orders to fall back. When neither came, he realized they could

not stay in their exposed position. All three Buckeye regiments suffered heavy casualties, with the 25th Ohio chalking up as many as 184 total losses out of their 220 men for a staggering 84% casualty rate.

Finding his division headed rearward, General Barlow was attempting to rally his men when he was shot in the left side. He dismounted and attempted to walk off the field. "Everybody was then running to the rear & the enemy was approaching rapidly," he wrote to his mother a few days later. Two men attempted to assist him until one was shot, and Barlow was then struck again with a spent bullet. Too faint to go any further, he lay down and another bullet grazed a finger as the Confederates continued to fire at his fleeing men. "I did not expect to get out alive." Finally, a staff officer that Barlow identified as belonging to General Early arrived and had him carried into the woods, placed on a bed of leaves, and provided with water.

Since Barlow was incapacitated, Adelbert Ames took command of the division's broken pieces. "The whole division was falling back with little or no regularity," Ames reported, "regimental organizations having become destroyed." Colonel von Gilsa also attempted in vain to rally the men. Ames soon received an order from Schurz to fall back through the town. As the men streamed past the almshouse property, some took refuge in the structures before being captured. "The Federal flank had been shriveled up as a scroll and the whole force gave way," is how Major Daniel of Jubal Early's staff later described the action.

Krzyzanowski's brigade had been placed on Barlow's left in a futile attempt to support and maintain a connection with Schimmelfennig. Kriz's men now faced a combined onslaught from Doles and Gordon. Moving astride the Carlisle Road,

Doles's men advanced in fine style until both sides opened fire at about 75 yards. Krzyzanowski rode his line and shouted orders as bullets whizzed about. A bullet struck his horse and threw him to the ground, but he remained on the field with his men. General Doles also lost control of his horse, which galloped straight for the enemy lines. Doles either fell or leapt to safety when only about 50 yards away and avoided serious injury.

Doles's right flank was temporarily threatened by the appearance of the 157th New York from von Amsberg's brigade. The New Yorkers received orders to assist Krzyzanowski and wheeled into the fields on the opposite side of the Carlisle Road. They opened fire when only about 30–40 yards from Doles's right. Several of Doles's regiments responded and poured in such a volley of fire that the Yankees were "not only checked but stampeded" in the words of one man. Schimmelfennig sent an aide to Colonel Philip Brown of the 157th with orders to retreat, but the staffer's horse was shot from under him, and the man only "hallooed" the order to Brown while walking to the rear. So, Colonel Brown ordered his own retreat.

Krzyzanowski's regiments were defeated with heavy losses. They suffered over 600 casualties, including more than 200 missing–captured, or 47% total losses for the battle. In comparison, Doles estimated only 219 losses for a 17% rate. Among the light Georgia casualties was Lieutenant Colonel David Winn of the 4th Georgia. Winn's body was buried on the Blocher property. In 1871, Winn's family wanted his corpse exhumed and reinterred back home. But David Blocher's adult son Oliver ransomed the body for $10 because Winn's skull possessed dental gold plating that Blocher valued. Rufus Weaver, who led the reburial effort, eventually paid $5

for Winn's remains, much to the disgust of the Georgian newspapers.

To Krzyzanowski's left, von Amsberg's brigade remained alone on the opposite side of the Carlisle Road. Having lost the effective services of the 157th New York, the remaining units withstood artillery fire from Oak Hill for much of the afternoon. By approximately 4:00 p.m., acting corps commander Schurz received word that Doubleday's First Corps was retreating due to renewed pressure on their front. At the same time, orders arrived from Howard for Schurz to withdraw to a position on Cemetery Hill. Dilger and Wheeler's batteries joined in the retreat, with Dilger firing a few canister rounds from the edge of town. Although it had not been an easy fight, Ewell's Second Corps had swept Schurz's Eleventh Corps from the ground north of Gettysburg, but more fighting remained to decide the day.

Since Robert E. Lee permitted a general advance in the afternoon, the attack along A. P. Hill's front to the west fell once again to Henry Heth's division. Among Heth's brigades, Colonel John Brockenbrough's Virginians advanced just south of Chambersburg Pike and toward Stone's position near the McPherson farm. Brockenbrough was 33 years old. He commanded his brigade as a colonel rather than a brigadier general without promotion since the wounding of Brigadier General Charles Field at Second Manassas in August 1862. Although Field's Virginians were battle-hardened veterans, they seemed to regress under uninspired leadership from Brockenbrough. They became disoriented at Fredericksburg and there were accusations of lax discipline after Chancellorsville.

As Brockenbrough's left regiments, the 55th and 47th Virginia, approached Willoughby's Run, they drove Stone's

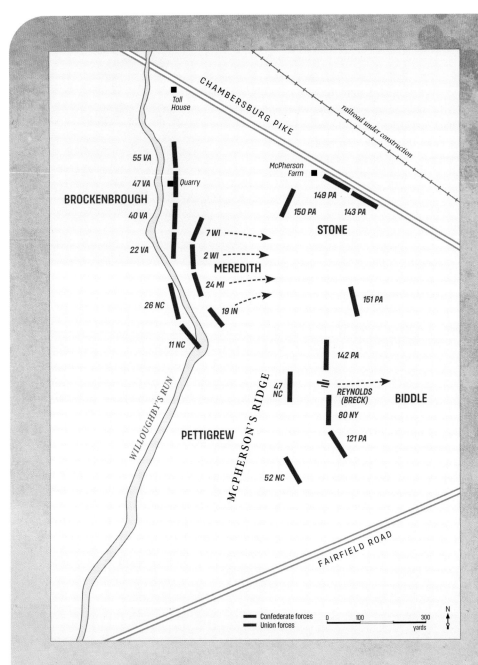

▲ Afternoon attack by Heth's division against First Corps on McPherson Ridge.

skirmishers back but were then confronted by the remnants of a quarry. Brockenbrough's men shifted to their right to bypass this obstacle and temporarily removed themselves from the fight.

The real strength of Heth's afternoon attack was delivered by the large brigade of more than 2,500 men under General Pettigrew. His four North Carolina regiments stepped off on Brockenbrough's right and advanced 500 yards across the Harmon farm to Willoughby's Run. While sweeping across the Harmon farm, soldiers set the family's house and barn on fire to deny them to Union skirmishers. They then splashed across the run and struck Doubleday's position on McPherson Ridge.

Pettigrew's left regiments, the 26th and 11th North Carolina, moved toward the Iron Brigade which had reformed in Herbst Woods after the morning's action. General Doubleday, uncertain of General Reynolds's intentions before the wing

◀ Gettysburg's citizen-warrior John Burns fought with the Iron Brigade and suffered several wounds. Burns recovered from his injuries, and photographs taken of his recuperation helped transform him into a national hero. (Gettysburg National Military Park)

commander was killed, doubled down on the defense of the woodlot. Despite the protests of Iron Brigade officers to shift into a more defensible position, Doubleday insisted on holding the ground. General Meredith's "Black Hats" realigned their regiments for the afternoon, such that

▼ This 1885 image shows the 19th Indiana regimental monument. The terrain is considerably more open in the photograph than it is today. Note Willoughby's Run to the front and the open landscape on the 19th Indiana's left. (Gettysburg National Military Park)

302—Willoughby's Run—(19th Ind. monument.)

▶ The Iron Brigade's 24th Michigan defended Herbst (sometimes referred to as Reynolds or McPherson) Woods on July 1 and suffered 363 total casualties, the highest numeric total of any Union regiment at Gettysburg. This circa-1897 monument image represents an enlisted man of the regiment loading his rifle while wearing the brigade's distinctive black hat. Note again the lack of undergrowth in the woods. (Gettysburg National Military Park)

the 19th Indiana held the brigade's left in vulnerable low ground south of the woods. To their right stood the 24th Michigan. The 2nd and 7th Wisconsin then formed the Iron Brigade's right and faced off against Brockenbrough's Virginians. Sometime during the day's fight, General Solomon Meredith suffered an injury when his horse was shot and fell on him. Command of the Iron Brigade then fell upon Colonel William Robinson of the 7th Wisconsin.

Around midday, 69-year-old local citizen John Burns approached the men of the 150th Pennsylvania. Dressed in a swallow-tailed coat and high hat while carrying a musket, the old man offered his services to the regiment. At Colonel Langhorne Wister's suggestion, Burns moved into the nearby woods and fell in with the 7th Wisconsin. Facing initial skepticism from the younger men, he allegedly shot a Rebel officer off his horse to prove his mettle. Burns then took position behind a tree and participated in the afternoon's battle with the Iron Brigade, suffering several wounds in the process.

Charles McConnell of the 24th Michigan observed the enemy's advance as slow, steady, and unchecked by Yankee fire. The Northerners opened fire as Pettigrew's men reached the banks of Willoughby's Run. The 11th North Carolina was a large regiment of about 600 men and led by Colonel Collett Leventhorpe, a 48-year-old native of England. The North Carolinians hit the 300 outnumbered men of the 19th Indiana and a fierce fight ensued. The Hoosiers' vulnerable left was outflanked, and Colonel Samuel Williams ordered his regiment's withdrawal to a second position about 100 yards to the rear. Williams's men struggled to hold this position too. The 19th Indiana's colors went down multiple times and as many as eight color bearers were killed or wounded getting off the field. Among these losses was Sergeant Major Asa Blanchard. No more than 20 years old, Blanchard attempted to rally the boys by waving the flag until a bullet severed an artery in his groin. Blanchard's last recorded words were, "Tell mother I never faltered."

◄ At 687 total casualties, the 26th North Carolina suffered more numeric losses than any Confederate regiment at Gettysburg. The regiment's colonel, Henry K. Burgwyn, Jr., was among them. This monument was dedicated in 1985 and is one of the more recent on the battlefield. (Author's photo)

To the right of the Hoosiers' original position, the 24th Michigan confronted the 26th North Carolina. The Southerners held the numeric advantage while the Yankees occupied their slightly elevated defensive position. Colonel Henry Morrow's 24th Michigan regiment was the newest addition to the Iron Brigade and fielded slightly fewer than 500 men. The 21-year-old Colonel Henry King Burgwyn led the 26th North Carolina. The "Boy Colonel" was a Virginia Military Institute graduate who received promotion to colonel and assumed command of the regiment in August 1862 when its prior colonel Zebulon Vance became governor of North Carolina. The 26th was the largest regiment in the Army of Northern Virginia with more than 800 men. These two above-average-sized regiments slugged it out on the eastern side of Willoughby's Run.

As the 26th North Carolina's advance up the eastern embankment stalled, several North Carolinian color bearers were struck down. Colonel Burgwyn seized the flag and started forward shouting, "Dress on the colors!" As he turned to give an order or hand the flag off to another volunteer, a ball tore through Burgwyn's side and knocked him to the ground. He died hours later.

Lieutenant Colonel John Lane took command of the regiment and pressed forward with the colors himself. "Twenty-sixth, follow me!" Eventually, they forced the 24th Michigan back to the eastern end of the woods. During this offensive, Lane was wounded while still carrying the colors. He survived, but it was believed to be the fourteenth time that the 26th North Carolina's colors fell during this assault. Shortly after the 24th retired, an officer from the brigade staff ordered the Wisconsin regiments to also fall back and

the Midwesterners began fighting their way backward toward the swale between McPherson and Seminary ridges.

Colonel Chapman Biddle's brigade from the First Corps Third Division deployed to the left of the 19th Indiana's original position, although there was a gap in between. Chapman Biddle hailed from a prominent Philadelphia family and practiced law prior to the war. (Colonel Biddle normally led the 121st Pennsylvania but assumed acting brigade command on July 1 when Brigadier General Thomas Rowley temporarily commanded the division.) Unlike the Iron Brigade, Biddle's men enjoyed little cover as their line extended south along McPherson Ridge. They complained about their exposed position to no avail.

Pettigrew's right regiments, the 47th and 52nd North Carolina, advanced against Biddle's brigade of fewer than 1,400 men. Waiting for the Confederates to approach, General Rowley rode up to his line and shouted, "Stand up for the Old Key Stone. There the Rebs are coming—give it to them!" The men replied with a shout. Unfortunately, Colonel James Marshall's 52nd North Carolina overlapped Biddle's left and forced the 121st Pennsylvania backwards.

The 47th North Carolina, meanwhile, hit the right and center of Biddle's line.

▲ Colonel Henry Burgwyn was appointed a Confederate officer in 1861 at only 19 years old. He was struck down on July 1 leading his 26th North Carolina regiment. (North Carolina Collection Photographic Archives, Wilson Library, UNC-Chapel Hill)

◄ Colonel Chapman Biddle had been a lawyer prior to the war. He was colonel of the 121st Pennsylvania Regiment but assumed brigade command at Gettysburg when General Rowley took over the division. Biddle received a head wound at Gettysburg but survived the battle and the war. (William Strong, *History of the 121st Regiment Pennsylvania Volunteers* [Philadelphia, 1906], 5)

Colonel Robert Cummins and his 142nd Pennsylvania counterattacked and temporarily stopped the Confederates. Cummins, a former county sheriff, was mortally wounded trying to rally his men around the regiment's flag. "The enemy were now advancing toward our position in line of battle," reported Colonel Theodore Gates of the 80th New York (also designated the 20th New York State Militia), "and the infantry fire became very severe." Gates saw friendly forces falling back on his right and left. Fearing being cut off, Gates took his regiment's flag from the color bearer and shouted for his men to stand by him. He then ordered a parting volley as the 20th started back toward Seminary Ridge along with the rest of Biddle's men.

Generals Doubleday and Rowley ordered their last reserve, the 151st Pennsylvania from Biddle's brigade, into the fray. Lieutenant Colonel George McFarland, a teacher and school principal who ran an academy in McAlisterville, Pennsylvania, raised a company of men when the regiment formed in late 1862. They were afterwards called "The Schoolteachers' Regiment" due to the large number of educators in the regiment. McFarland led the regiment at Gettysburg because the colonel was absent due to illness.

McFarland's men were ordered to cover the gap that existed between the left of the hard-pressed Iron Brigade and Biddle's right. This placed the regiment near the southeast corner of Herbst Woods. McFarland had often insisted on target practice for his men while in camp and he now told them to take deliberate aim rather than unleashing volleys of gunfire. The 151st made a gallant but futile stand. "Men fell thick and fast in our front," McFarland recalled. As the Iron Brigade passed by, the surging

Confederates hit the 151st with a severe fire. Since both flanks were threatened, the schoolteachers were caught in what appeared to be a crossfire. After seeing no friendly supports, McFarland ordered his men to retire while firing toward the Lutheran Seminary.

Although Doubleday's line was pushed off McPherson Ridge, Heth's attack stalled near the eastern edge of the woods due to increasing casualties, exhaustion, and low ammunition. Pettigrew led Heth's assault and suffered perhaps 1,000 casualties as reward for their victory, the brunt being in the 11th and 26th North Carolina regiments. General Heth was among the casualties. A spent Minie ball struck him in the head, but Heth's hat was too large, and he had stuffed papers inside to make it fit. The papers deflected the bullet and likely avoided a more serious wound. As it was, Heth was knocked unconscious and out of the remainder of the battle.

Meanwhile on Oak Ridge, General Baxter's tired men were running low on

▼ After his 151st Pennsylvania Regiment withdrew from McPherson Ridge to Seminary Ridge, former educator Lieutenant Colonel George McFarland suffered wounds which resulted in the loss of one of his legs. McFarland did not leave the hospital established in the Seminary's main building for another two and a half months. (Charles Robson, ed., *Biographical Encyclopedia of Pennsylvania in the Nineteenth Century* [Philadelphia, 1874], 662)

ammunition and Robinson replaced them with Brigadier General Gabriel Paul's brigade of about 1,500 men. The 50-year-old Paul was a West Point graduate and career army officer. Despite 27 years of pre-Civil War experience, Paul only received promotion to brigadier general in late 1862 after his wife lobbied President Lincoln about her husband's experience. The new brigadier and his five regiments joined General Robinson's division only shortly before Gettysburg.

General Paul's brigade now anchored the right of Doubleday's First Corps, but was in an awkward position. Not only did the gap remain between the First Corps right and the Eleventh Corps left on the plain below, but Paul's own left fronted to the west while his right curved to the right and faced the Mummasburg Road. His position faced in two directions and looked like an inverted "V."

Paul defended Oak Ridge against the next attempt from Brigadier General Stephen Ramsuer's brigade. The North Carolina native was an aggressive fighter and another emerging leader within the Army of Northern Virginia. An ambitious West Point graduate, he eagerly volunteered when war started. Ramseur was promoted to brigadier general in November 1862 while recovering from a mangled arm suffered at Malvern Hill, making the 25-year-old the youngest Confederate general at that time. His brigade incurred 50% casualties at

▲ Brigadier General Gabriel Paul's brigade was the last to defend Oak Ridge against the Confederate assaults. Paul received a severe head wound, and he suffered from the effects of it for the remainder of his life. (Warner, *Generals in Blue*, 363)

◄ North Carolina native Brigadier General Stephen "Dod" Ramseur was one of the youngest officers on the battlefield. An inspiring battlefield presence, Ramseur led the final and successful assault against Oak Ridge. (Library of Congress)

Chancellorsville, the highest in Lee's army, but he won more praise from superiors. Despite his youth, Ramseur appeared as an inspiring presence who enjoyed the excitement of battle.

Rodes ordered Ramseur to send two of his regiments, the 2nd and 4th North Carolina, toward their left to support O'Neal. His other two regiments, the 30th and 14th North Carolina, were placed on the right to assist Iverson. Coming upon the field, Ramseur "found three regiments of Iverson's command almost annihilated," and the 3rd Alabama coming out of the fight. Ramsuer requested the regiment's colonel to join him, which he "cheerfully" did. With this jumble of commands, Ramseur made a final push against Paul's salient on Oak Ridge.

Ramseur's men double-quicked down slope from Oak Hill. One of his colonels called out to Ramseur requesting they swing left and envelop the enemy. General Ramseur replied, "No, let's go directly in upon them." Ramseur was a skilled horseman and led the charge mounted, despite only being able to use one arm.

A Union soldier shot Ramseur's mount as they neared the wall on Oak Ridge but missed the general.

On the Union side, General Robinson insisted that his commanders remain on horseback to provide visible leadership. Robinson had two horses shot out from under him, but he emerged unharmed. General Paul was not as lucky. The old veteran received a wound early in the fight while riding behind his lines. A bullet struck him in the right temple and exited through his left eye socket. He survived until 1886 but suffered greatly because of his Gettysburg wound.

According to Robinson, it was nearly 5:00 p.m. when he received orders to withdraw. The 16th Maine, whose Colonel William Tilden claimed that he had fewer than 200 men in ranks at this point, were ordered by Robinson to cover the division's retreat and hold their position "as long as there was a man left." Tilden's men posted their colors near the junction of Oak Ridge's stone wall and the Mummasburg Road. When Robinson repeated, "take the position and hold it

◀ This 1890s image shows the portion of Robinson's Oak Ridge position on the left that faced toward the Mummasburg Road, which runs through the photo. The War Department's Oak Ridge observation tower is in the background. (Gettysburg National Military Park)

▶ The 16th Maine's advance marker facing the Mummasburg Road. The regiment was ordered to hold this position at any cost while the brigade retreated from Oak Ridge. (Author's photo)

at any cost," Tilden could only inform his men "you know what that means."

The two sides exchanged gunfire as Ramseur's regiments appeared. The Maine men took hits in their front and flank. Despite Robinson's admonishments, the regiment fell back firing and likely did not delay the Rebels for long. With Tilden's permission, however, the regiment's color bearers tore their flags into pieces too small to be captured as trophies. As Robinson's men abandoned the field, Ramseur described how the Federals "ran off the field in confusion, leaving his killed and wounded and between 800 and 900 prisoners in our hands." After multiple attempts that nearly chewed up Robert Rodes's division, the Confederates finally captured Oak Ridge. To what advantage remained to be seen.

Retreat to Cemetery Hill

The Army of the Potomac forcibly retreated through town and toward Cemetery Hill after fierce day-long fighting. The narrow streets of Gettysburg and the separation of individual regiments created confusion as soldiers attempted to reach the rallying point.

General Doubleday reported afterwards that it was about 4:00 p.m. when the enemy's advance "having been strongly re-enforced, advanced in large numbers." His First Corps had fought and delayed the Confederate momentum without reinforcements since mid-morning. There were no remaining reserves among his exhausted men. A retreat became necessary.

The Eleventh Corps was unable to provide any additional help. General Howard's determination to hold Cemetery Hill as a "last resort" resulted in his holding one remaining division under General Adolph von Steinwehr in reserve on Cemetery Hill. Howard was reluctant to initially release any of von Steinwehr's division to answer Schurz's repeated calls for support. "Hold out, if possible, awhile longer," Howard replied to reinforcement appeals, "for I am expecting General Slocum every moment." But Lee's army was advancing again from multiple directions and there was still no Slocum.

Howard finally permitted use of Colonel Adolphus Buschbeck's brigade to cover the retreat through town. This small brigade of four regiments had earned praise for standing against Jackson's attack at Chancellorsville. Buschbeck was absent at Gettysburg, and Colonel Charles Coster of the 134th New York led the brigade instead.

Coster's 134th New York, 154th New York, and 27th Pennsylvania deployed behind a fence near John Kuhn's brickyard on Stratton Street at the northern edge of town. (Coster's fourth regiment, the 73rd Pennsylvania, was held back as a reserve.) Coster's men were hardly in position when two Confederate brigades in Jubal Early's division attacked. Coming in behind Gordon's brigade which had smashed Barlow at Blocher's Knoll, Brigadier General Harry Hays's "Louisiana Tigers" of about 1,300 men advanced partially on the north side of the Harrisburg Road. They hit the 27th Pennsylvania and a battery of Napoleons under Captain Lewis Heckman on Coster's left. Meanwhile, Colonel Isaac Avery's 1,200 North Carolinians were to the left of Hays and moved against Coster's right.

General Hays described his men being struck with "unusually galling" artillery

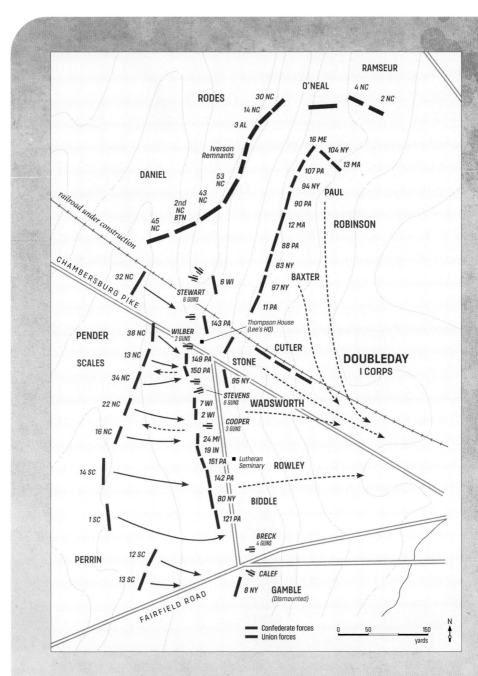

▲ Confederate attacks against Seminary and Oak ridges.

fire but his advance was "rapid and impetuous" as they suffered small losses. Hays's Tigers turned Coster's left and the 27th Pennsylvania retreated. Heckman's artillery fire from their position near the Carlisle Road was partially blocked by retreating Eleventh Corps troops in their front. Nevertheless, the battery fired up to 113 rounds in about 30 minutes of action before the Confederates overran and captured two Napoleons.

Coster's other two regiments, the 154th New York in the center and 134th New York on the right, were unaware of this withdrawal and continued to fight. The combat here was fiercer than on Coster's left. Colonel Archibald Godwin of the 57th North Carolina in Avery's brigade reported receiving destructive gunfire and canister after crossing Rock Creek about 200 yards from Coster's line. "Colonel Avery now gave the order to double-quick, and the brigade gallantly dashed through the stream and up the hill to the fence, the enemy stubbornly holding their position until we had climbed over into their midst."

Coster's men opened fire, but the 134th New York's right was in the air. Avery's men turned it so thoroughly that they were soon behind the New Yorkers, enfiladed the entire line, and forced them back from

▲ Brigadier General Harry Hays was born in Tennessee, served in the Mexican War, and had been employed as a prominent lawyer in New Orleans. Hays was promoted to brigadier general in July 1862, and his "Louisiana Tigers" enjoyed a hard-fighting reputation within the army. (Library of Congress)

◄ This 1890s image of the 154th New York regimental monument shows the position they defended in the brickyard near Stratton Street. An open landscape and the buildings of Gettysburg are visible in the distance, which is strikingly different to how it looks in the present day. (Gettysburg National Military Park)

▲ A modern image of Coster Avenue, as part of the defensive line held briefly by Coster's brigade before they were overwhelmed. Monuments to the 154th New York (left) and 27th Pennsylvania (right) are visible. A mural by artist Mark Dunkelman illustrates the brickyard fight and adorns the post-war commercial building behind the monuments. (Author's photo)

▶ The monument to Battery K, 1st Ohio Light Artillery, sits on the north side of Gettysburg and on what is today part of the Gettysburg College campus. Captain Lewis Heckman only assumed command of the battery in mid-May. This image is from the 1890s; the college campus behind the battery has changed considerably since then. (Gettysburg National Military Park)

the fence. The 134th New York suffered 42 killed and 151 wounded, the largest number of those categories in Coster's brigade by a wide margin. Seeing both the right and left turned, the commander of the 154th New York also ordered his regiment to withdraw.

Confusion reigned as Coster's men fled back into Stratton Street, pursued by both Avery and Hays's troops. Hand-to-hand conflict ensued. "The enemy now fled into the town," Colonel Godwin of the 57th North Carolina reported, "many of them being killed in the retreat." Among

those killed was Sergeant Amos Humiston of the 154th New York. His unidentified corpse was discovered afterwards with a photo of three children clutched in his hand. A nationwide search commenced in newspapers to identify this soldier and his children. Later that fall, Philinda Humiston of Portville, New York, identified the family as hers.

Coster's brigade incurred more than 550 casualties along with the loss of Heckman's two Napoleons. General Schurz credited their sacrifice as having allowed time for Barlow's division to escape through town, yet at a tremendous cost. More than 300 men in the brigade became prisoners of war, and many of them died in captivity as additional casualties of Gettysburg's first day.

Along Doubleday's front on the crumbling Union left, a German staff officer instructed Colonel Charles Wainwright, commanding the First Corps Artillery Brigade, to hold Cemetery Hill at all hazards. "What with the aide's broken English and our being on this hill and not knowing there was a cemetery, I thought it was the Seminary Hill we were to hold. I had therefore strung my batteries out on it as well as I could." The upshot of Wainwright's confusion was that the First Corps deployed a formidable artillery line along Seminary Ridge that would delay

▲ The 5th Maine Battery under Captain Greenlief Stevens was one of several Union batteries that defended Seminary Ridge against Confederate assaults in the late afternoon. Trees which were not present at the time of battle now obscure some of the view, but the Southerners attacked from McPherson Ridge in the background while under fire from batteries stretched along much of the ridge. (Author's photo)

▶ The monument to the 143rd Pennsylvania was erected in 1889 near the Chambersburg Pike. It shows Sergeant Ben Crippen shaking his fist at advancing Confederates. Crippen was killed during the regiment's retreat, and his body was never recovered. (Photo by Phil Spaugy)

the next round of Confederate attacks. As many as 15 artillery pieces deployed from the Chambersburg Pike to the Fairfield Road, while six more guns were north of the pike and another five unlimbered south of the road on the left of the line.

Doubleday's infantry fell back to Seminary Ridge in some disorder. The general had earlier ordered the construction of breastworks on the western side of the seminary buildings. The Iron Brigade manned these fortifications and took position to the left of Captain Greenlief Stevens's 5th Maine, Battery E. Colonel Biddle's men then took position to the left of this line, but theirs ended just south of the main seminary building and stopped short of the Fairfield Road. Some of John Buford's cavalry in Gamble's brigade and Calef's battery were placed

south of the Fairfield Road to protect Doubleday's extreme left flank, but a gap existed between Biddle and Gamble.

The Bucktails were among the last to retreat from McPherson Ridge and arrive on Doubleday's Seminary Ridge line. British military observer Lieutenant Colonel Arthur Fremantle watched the action from a ridgetop with Lee and A. P. Hill. General Hill commented that he had been unwell all day but professed his admiration for a Northern color bearer who "retired last of all, turning round every now and then to shake his fist at the advancing rebels." Hill was sorry to see "the gallant Yankee meet his doom." The veterans of the 143rd Pennsylvania later identified this as Sergeant Benjamin Crippen, and their battlefield monument represents his likeness shaking his fist in perpetuity. (Not everyone agreed. The 150th Pennsylvania veterans identified Hill's fist-shaking Yankee as Sergeant Samuel Peiffer, who was also killed that day.)

Major General William Dorsey Pender's division followed behind Heth's division with the next Confederate assault wave. The 29-year-old North Carolinian and West Point graduate was another rising star in the Army of Northern Virginia, having excelled as a brigade commander while being wounded in action several times. Pender received promotion and command of A. P. Hill's famed Light Division upon the latter's elevation to Third Corps command. Lee heartily endorsed Pender's promotion and reportedly declared him as the most promising young officer in the army. Pender's division was large at about 6,600 men. The brigades under Colonel Abner Perrin and brigadier generals James Lane and Alfred Scales were ready for action, although a fourth brigade under Brigadier General Edward Thomas was held out of the fight in reserve supporting artillery.

▼ Major General William Dorsey Pender was another of the many recently promoted officers. Leading a division in A. P. Hill's Third Corps, Pender's men made the final attack against Doubleday on Seminary Ridge. (Library of Congress)

General Pender probably intended a coordinated attack by his three brigades. On the left was the brigade under Alfred Scales, a 35-year-old politician who received brigade command when Pender was promoted to lead the division. General Scales's North Carolina regiments initiated their assault with enthusiasm and their approach caused the remainder of Stone's brigade to withdraw from McPherson Ridge. The Tar Heels passed over remnants of Heth's division, likely Brockenbrough's brigade, whose men informed Scales's officers they were out of ammunition and could go no further. As Scales pressed forward into the swale between McPherson and Seminary ridges, however, they were hit directly with shell and canister from the enemy batteries on Seminary Ridge at distances of less than 200 yards. From there, Scales's men could neither advance nor retreat safely as enemy projectiles tore great gaps in their lines. General Scales was among the wounded, along with a large portion of the brigade's nearly 1,400 men.

The advance of Pender's right was also obstructed. Gamble's cavalry and Calef's battery posted just south of the Fairfield Road threatened Pender's right brigade under Brigadier General James Lane. Fearing a mounted attack from Gamble's cavalrymen, Lane temporarily halted his men and refused his right. When they advanced again, Lane's men drifted to the right and widened a gap with the rest of Pender's line, effectively removing themselves from the fight.

Due to Scales and Lane's difficulties, the brunt of the Confederate attack against Seminary Ridge fell to Colonel Abner Perrin's brigade of South Carolinians. Abner Perrin proved himself to be one of the day's unsung heroes for the Army of Northern Virginia. The 36-year-old former

lawyer fought in many of the Eastern Theater's prior battles but commanded a regiment only once previously: the 14th South Carolina at Chancellorsville. Perrin also temporarily led the brigade near the close of Chancellorsville when its commander Samuel McGowan received a severe wound. McGowan was not ready to return for the Gettysburg campaign, so Colonel Perrin retained brigade command. The men of his brigade were proud and experienced, but Perrin was an unknown commodity at this level as they went into action.

Advancing toward the seminary with four regiments, Perrin ordered his men to press forward and close with the enemy. They were not to stop and fire until instructed to do so. Perrin did not

▲ Brigadier General Alfred Scales's North Carolina brigade suffered heavy casualties from Union artillery on Seminary Ridge. General Scales was among the wounded and was unable to participate when the brigade also took part in the famed "Pickett–Pettigrew–Trimble Charge" on July 3. (Library of Congress)

▶ Colonel Abner Perrin's brigade followed Scales in assaulting Seminary Ridge. Perrin's men hit Doubleday's line in front and flank, causing the Northern forces to retreat. (Warner, *Generals in Gray*, 235)

led a charge. A lieutenant noted the brigade followed "with a shout that was itself half a victory." As the lieutenant colonel of the 14th South Carolina observed, "to stop was destruction. To retreat was disaster. To go forward was orders." Perrin directed his 1st South Carolina to outflank the Northerners at the gap in Doubleday's defenses south of the seminary's main building, between Biddle and Gamble's positions. The 14th South Carolina then hit the Northerners' front. Biddle's line collapsed and his men fell back, although nearby Federal batteries limbered up and escaped before the Southerners could capture them.

Lieutenant Colonel McFarland of the 151st Pennsylvania estimated they resisted the Confederate assault for "ten or more minutes." In other words, not very long. As Perrin's South Carolinians were outflanking them, McFarland led about 100 of his men toward the north side of the seminary building. While there, he was wounded in the legs by a volley. A soldier carried McFarland through the north door of the building while the enemy entered the same structure through the

want his men to stand and shoot instead of charging. His left regiment, the 14th South Carolina, struggled under some of the same fire that stopped Scales. Yankee infantry also fired away from near their barricade. As many as 34 of 39 men in the 14th's Company K were said to have been shot down in front of the seminary lines.

With his assault potentially wavering, Perrin saw the need for a display of personal leadership. He urged his horse forward and

▶ The railroad cut looking east from post-battle Reynolds Avenue, circa 1885. Oak Ridge (to the left) and Seminary Ridge (right) are visible. Union soldiers retreated through the cut toward Gettysburg, which is visible in the distance. (Gettysburg National Military Park)

south door. The regiment then began their retreat toward Cemetery Hill without him. McFarland survived and received medical care in the building for more than two months as one leg required amputation below the knee.

General Wadsworth told Captain Stevens to withdraw his 5th Maine, Battery E, but Colonel Wainwright initially countermanded the order under the continued mistaken impression they still intended to defend Seminary Ridge. They then observed, however, other Union divisions such as Robinson's retreating over the railroad cut and so Wainwright ordered his First Corps batteries to limber up and get out.

The unfinished railroad that cut through Oak Ridge and headed east toward town became a primary avenue of escape for First Corps troops. Lieutenant James

Stewart's 4th United States, Battery B and supporting infantry had defended the cut during the afternoon. Stewart extracted his battery through the rock-filled cut with great difficulty. At one point, a party of Rebels dashed within 50–60 yards and killed one driver while seriously wounding another. Stewart's 36 total losses were the second highest suffered by any Union battery during the battle, but he eventually reached Cemetery Hill.

"We had the Yankees like partridges in a nest," wrote one veteran from Ramseur's brigade, "and the only way they could get out was up the railroad." This may have been the largest mass capture of Union troops during the battle. Lieutenant Colonel William Lewis of the 43rd North Carolina described the action at the railroad cut where "400 or 500 prisoners surrendered to the brigade; also

▼ Modern view of the intersection at Washington and High streets. Catherine Foster's residence is in the background. At day's end, fighting occurred in these streets as the First and Eleventh Corps retreated to Cemetery Hill. (Author's photo)

▶ Brigadier General Thomas Rowley's behavior during the retreat to Cemetery Hill led to allegations that he was drunk on duty. Rowley was convicted by a court martial but reinstated and reassigned to a district command in Western Pennsylvania. (Library of Congress)

several stands of colors were captured." Colonel William Hoffman of the 56th Pennsylvania described Wadsworth's men moving over the railroad bed and colliding with the retreating 11th Corps troops at Baltimore Street as the roads began to converge in town. This stopped their momentum and caused the capture of men at the rear.

Earlier that morning, the citizens of Gettysburg had watched with hope as their Union defenders passed through town to meet their opponents. By late afternoon, the locals became alarmed by the increasing numbers of wounded, fugitive soldiers, and wagons that were returning from the day's battlefields in increasing haste. Public buildings and private homes were pressed into service as hospitals. After 4:00 p.m., officers arrived and cried out for women and children to take to their cellars as the Rebels were likely to shell the town and engage in house-to-house fighting.

Fortunately for the noncombatants, these threats did not materialize.

Both Doubleday and Schurz insisted that their men had not succumbed to a panic-stricken rout. There is no evidence, however, that anyone was able to manage and organize the masses as they withdrew through the town. One captain recalled hearing shouts of "First Corps this way" and "Eleventh Corps this way" but was unclear of what was expected. Colonel Wainwright saw little organization but described the First Corps men walking on one side of the street while the Eleventh took to the other. Far from being panic-stricken, most seemed to be talking or joking. One of Cutler's aides described artillery passing in the streets while infantry walked along sides.

Schurz acknowledged that there were many stragglers behaving in a disorderly fashion, but that was expected in such a situation. Schurz thought disorder primarily existed where the mass of wagons blocked the town's streets. Lieutenant Colonel Edward Salomon of the 82nd Illinois found considerable confusion and considered it a rout. Rout or not, many units were clearly on their own and lost organization as they made individual attempts to reach Cemetery Hill.

Numerous casualties at the brigade and regimental levels compounded Howard and Doubleday's issues. The possible drunkenness of Doubleday's temporary Third Division commander Brigadier General Thomas Rowley also proved troublesome. While passing through town, Rowley had a brief verbal altercation with General Cutler and then attempted to override Doubleday's orders in placing some of Cutler's men. When confronted, Rowley replied that he "did not care a damn for General Doubleday." Rowley thought he commanded the First

Street Fighting in Gettysburg

Although fears of mass combat in the town did not materialize, confusion and hostilities still played out in Gettysburg's streets, alleyways, and homes.

Young Anna Garlach thought the streets so crowded with soldiers that she could have crossed them by stepping on men's heads. Catherine Foster observed Union soldiers on Washington Street ducking into corners to dodge bullets as they hurried for safety. Henry Jacobs witnessed a Union soldier being shot dead as he ran frantically from Confederate pursuers. Colonel Wheelock of the 97th New York was nearly killed in Carrie Sheads's academy on Chambersburg Street when he refused to surrender his sword to a Rebel sergeant. Carrie saved the day by hiding the sword in the folds of her skirt when the Southerner was distracted. From his basement window at Baltimore and High streets, Albertus McCreary saw a Union cannon fire down Baltimore Street and create a great commotion.

As the 45th New York withdrew toward Cemetery Hill, they found their route blocked on Washington Street, so they cut through the alleys near Christ Lutheran Church on Chambersburg Street instead. Captain Francis Irsch and four companies in the rear took shelter in buildings opposite the Church and intended to fight it out. They held out until about 5:30 p.m. when Confederates convinced Irsch the town was in their possession and induced him to surrender.

Christ Lutheran Church was among the many public buildings converted into field hospitals and overflowing with arrivals of more wounded. Chaplain Horatio Howell of the 90th Pennsylvania was among those tending to the wounded there. The street noise drew Howell out from the Church and onto the large stairs in front. Accounts vary in detail, but a Southern soldier might have called upon Howell to surrender his sword. The chaplain refused under the premise that he was a non-combatant and a Confederate shot Howell dead.

Near the corner of Washington and High streets, members of the 150th Pennsylvania exchanged gunfire with some of Ramseur's North Carolinians. Corporal Joseph Gutelius was killed while carrying the 150th's flag. Lieutenant Frank Harney of the 14th North Carolina captured the Pennsylvanian's flag before being mortally wounded. As his dying wish,

▲ Christ Evangelical Lutheran Church's exterior has not changed significantly since this early 1900s photo. It was one of the town's first public buildings pressed into service as a hospital. Chaplain Horatio Howell of the 90th Pennsylvania was shot and killed while standing on the church's stairs. A small plaque commemorating Howell is visible at the bottom of the steps. (Gettysburg National Military Park)

Harney requested the captured colors be sent to Confederate President Jefferson Davis. Several weeks later, Davis confirmed the flag was in his possession, "and will be treasured by me as an honorable memento of the valor and patriotism and devotion which the soldiers of North Carolina have displayed on many hard-fought fields." The flag remained with Davis and was among his personal belongings when he was captured in 1865 at the end of the war.

General Alexander Schimmelfennig also endeavored to reach the safety of Cemetery Hill. After his horse was shot from under him, he climbed a fence into the yard of Henry and Catherine Garlach. Schimmelfennig crawled under a covered drainage ditch in the yard and escaped detection. After dark, he repositioned himself and hid near a woodshed between a stack of firewood and a hog swill barrel. Mrs. Garlach discovered the general that night when she went into her yard to slop her hogs. She continued to feed him the following day while pretending to feed her pigs. Schimmelfennig remained hidden in the yard until the morning of July 4, when he rejoined his men after the Confederates withdrew from town.

Corps "and would put the troops where he pleased." Rowley subsequently fell from his horse and continued to behave in an excited manner, giving wild orders before finally being placed under arrest. Several officers testified at the ensuing court martial that they assumed Rowley was intoxicated. (Although others testified that they did not consider him drunk.) Rowley replied in defense that he was sick, not a good horseman, and assumed that he commanded the First Corps while Doubleday led Reynolds's wing. Rowley's court martial convicted him, but his dismissal was not upheld, and he received reassignment to a district command in western Pennsylvania.

Carry the Hill, if Practicable

Richard Ewell's Second Corps had a successful day, but critical decisions still awaited Ewell and Lee as the first day ended. Meanwhile, Union generals Howard, Hancock, and others worked to strengthen Cemetery Hill while awaiting more reinforcements.

Oliver Howard's decision to commit his Eleventh Corps to a weak position north of Gettysburg, rather than pulling his and Doubleday's corps back to a more defensible position, was likely predicated on the false assumption that he would be reinforced by Henry Slocum's Twelfth Corps at Two Taverns (five miles away) or Dan Sickles's Third Corps at Emmitsburg (ten miles away). "Had we received re-enforcements a little sooner," Howard reported, "the first position assumed by General Reynolds, and held by General Doubleday till my corps came up, might have been maintained."

During the afternoon, Howard sent messages to both Slocum and Sickles requesting that they move up to his assistance. Unfortunately, both generals were conflicted by prior orders. Sickles had been told initially to maintain his position at Emmitsburg and subsequently also likely received Meade's Pipe Creek Circular, which would have moved his corps to Middleburg, Maryland.

In Slocum's case, he probably received the Pipe Creek Circular in the early afternoon with instructions to "halt your command where this order reaches you." There is evidence that Slocum started for Gettysburg with Brigadier General

▼ Major General Henry Slocum commanded the Army of the Potomac's Twelfth Corps and was expected to take charge of the battlefield from Howard. For reasons that are still debated, Slocum did not reach the field until early evening. (Library of Congress)

Alpheus Williams's division as early as 2:00 p.m. upon receiving reports of fighting there. He still took several hours to reach Cemetery Hill, however, and there is speculation that Slocum resisted taking charge of another potential Chancellorsville-like mess from General Howard. Around 4:00 p.m., Major Charles Howard (the general's brother) met Slocum about one mile from Gettysburg with a request to come up. Slocum replied that he had divisions on his flanks but did not wish to take responsibility for the fight. Slocum later told Hancock's chief of staff

that he did not want to be accountable for affairs over "which he had no control." Slocum arrived after the fighting was over and assumed command of Cemetery Hill as the senior officer. Howard noted that Slocum "afterward expressed the opinion that it was against the wish of the commanding general to bring on a general engagement at that point," which can be chalked up as one potential impact of the Pipe Creek Circular.

Howard received credit and vindication, however, for selecting Cemetery Hill as his rallying point. It formed an excellent

▶ Although General Oliver Howard does not always enjoy the highest reputation among Civil War military historians, his establishing Cemetery Hill as the Army of the Potomac's rallying point contributed significantly toward ultimate victory. (Author's photo)

position that later served as the "hook" in General Meade's so-called fishhook defense. The gentle slopes and fields of fire to the east and west suited Union artillery. The stone walls that crisscrossed the hill provided shelter for defending infantry. Cemetery Hill also controlled access to or from Gettysburg via two roads: Baltimore Pike and the Taneytown Road. Both roads were important as the Army of the Potomac was still approaching Gettysburg from the south and would likewise retreat in that direction in the event of disaster. The Baltimore Pike, as an improved or macadamized road, assumed increased significance for George Meade's supply and communications after Meade established his supply base near Westminster, Maryland. Such concerns were, however, primarily in the future. For now, Oliver Howard and Abner Doubleday needed to rally their defeated and disorganized troops against a foe seemingly in pursuit.

Officers such as the 6th Wisconsin's Rufus Dawes understandably saw disorder when they arrived. One First Corps officer allegedly stood by while directing troops with, "First Corps to the right and Eleventh Corps go to hell." Despite tensions between the two corps, and animosity that flared between Doubleday and Howard afterwards when each painted the best portrayal of his own performance, the two men worked to restore order.

General Winfield S. Hancock's arrival materially assisted the rallying on Cemetery Hill. Described as "excited" vs. Howard's "cool," participants noted Hancock's energy and commanding presence. Having spent the afternoon travelling from Taneytown at Meade's orders, Hancock was to assume command and determine if Gettysburg was a suitable place to concentrate the army and fight. Hancock ranked below Howard in

seniority, however, and although Meade had authority to elevate or replace anyone whom he deemed proper, Hancock knew the situation could be troublesome if Howard protested it.

Accounts varied afterwards regarding Howard's reaction to Hancock's arrival. Hancock reported that he assumed command while the First and Eleventh were retiring through the town. While the position was "already partially occupied" by Howard's direction, "vigorous efforts" caused a formidable line to be established. In this, Hancock acknowledged the "material assistance" of Howard, Buford, Warren, and others.

Howard wrote Meade at 5:00 p.m. that Hancock arrived an hour earlier "and communicated his instructions." Yet, Howard wrote later that he did not receive the written orders for Hancock to take over until 7:00 p.m. and command turned over, at that time, to the senior General Slocum.

Captain Eminel Halstead of Doubleday's staff wrote that Hancock offered to show Howard the order placing him in command. Howard declined, saying he did not doubt Hancock's word but, "You can give no orders here while I am here." Hancock accepted this and agreed to second any orders Howard gave rather than argue over protocol. Both men agreed that this was a strong position. "We agreed at once that that was no time for talking," Howard reported, "and that General Hancock should further arrange the troops, and place the batteries upon the left of the Baltimore pike, while I should take the right of the same."

While they subsequently worked professionally to defend Cemetery Hill, there is no doubt Howard's pride was wounded as he wrote Meade that evening, "The above has mortified me and will disgrace me. Please inform me frankly if you disapprove of my conduct to-day, that I may know what to do." Unfortunately for Doubleday, Howard also passed along to Hancock that "Doubleday's command gave way." Hancock dutifully passed this information on to Meade. The existing communications suggest General Meade already likely decided to replace Doubleday as First Corps commander with Major General John Newton, so the Howard–Hancock–Meade communication was not the cause as many historians assume, but it was an unfair slight against Doubleday's performance which the New Yorker rightfully resented.

Hancock made important dispositions that discouraged the Confederates on July 1 and paid dividends in the days ahead. Hancock directed Captain Stevens's battery of six Napoleons toward a small knoll between Cemetery and Culp's hills that now bears Stevens's name. This strengthened a potentially troublesome gap between the two hills. Hancock acknowledged the Cemetery Hill position "cannot well be taken. It is a position, however, easily turned." Slocum's pending arrival would protect the right and

Hancock also sent portions of Wadsworth's First Corps to Culp's Hill.

As Brigadier General John Geary's Twelfth Corps division began their arrival ahead of General Slocum, Hancock instructed Geary that "the immediate need of a division on the left was imperative." Geary extended his First and Third brigades "to a range of hills south and west of the town … These hills I regarded as of the utmost importance, since their possession by the enemy would give him an opportunity of enfilading our entire left wing and center with a fire which could not fail to dislodge us from our position." These hills on the left, including Little Round Top, played a critical part in the next day's battle.

No one knows the actual troop strength of this Cemetery Hill position, but perhaps 7,000 soldiers manned Cemetery Hill and parts of Culp's Hill before reinforcements arrived. The artillery was the key, however, with approximately 40 pieces fronting west, north, and northeast. The Southerners would pay for any direct assault on this position, but as it turns out their own momentum also stalled in the streets of Gettysburg during these hours.

▶ This 1863 image shows Culp's Hill from East Cemetery Hill along the Baltimore Pike. Culp's Hill could have dominated the pike and Cemetery Hill if occupied, but Ewell's forces failed to seize it. (Gettysburg National Military Park)

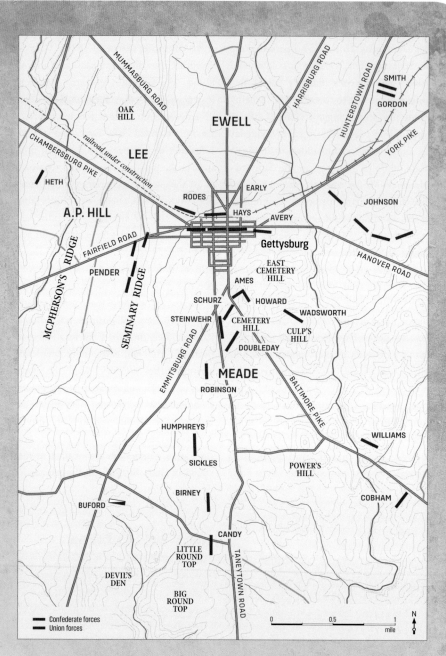

▲ Union fishhook position forming on Cemetery Hill and Culp's Hill. Confederate advances stall to the north and west.

▶ The gatehouse to the local Evergreen Cemetery. This image was taken shortly after the battle from East Cemetery Hill. Some of the cemetery's headstones are visible in the left background. (Gettysburg National Military Park)

The success of Ewell's Second Corps during this afternoon had not allowed time to plan the next steps. Lee previously warned against bringing on a general engagement before the army concentrated. Pushing a defeated opponent was an expected outcome, but Ewell's men fought hard and on the offense all afternoon, suffered their own casualties, and were further disorganized by the narrow streets of Gettysburg. As General Doles commented in his report, the Southerners failed to cut off the Federal retreat simply because the enemy "retired faster than we advanced." Even Ewell took some physical lumps. By one account, he was unhorsed by an artillery projectile, and General Gordon later described the corps commander being struck in his artificial leg by Yankee Minie balls. Fortunately, Ewell assured Gordon, "It don't hurt a bit to be shot in a wooden leg." Despite all these factors, General Ewell still had tough decisions ahead of him before this day ended.

What exactly happened is colored by the memories and motives of the participants, many of which were fitted to blame Ewell afterwards. As Ewell and his subordinates entered town from the north, they could see the Northerners reforming on Cemetery Hill. Every minute bought time for the enemy to reorganize. Generals Rodes and Early strongly urged continuing the attack, although both also requested support from A. P. Hill's Third Corps. Yet, Early's division was reduced by the detachment of "Extra Billy" Smith's brigade to watch against reports of enemy moving near the York Pike (possibly a sighting of Williams's Twelfth Corps division). After several warnings, Early eventually sent Gordon and his brigade to take charge of the situation, leaving Early short by two of his four brigades. At the same time, none of Rodes's troops could be considered "fresh" at this hour.

Lee sent his chief aide-de-camp, Walter Taylor, with orders to Ewell. "I received a message from the commanding general to attack this hill," Ewell reported, "if I could do so to advantage." Likewise, Lee reported that Ewell was "instructed to carry the hill occupied by the enemy, if he found it practicable, but to avoid a general engagement until the arrival of the other divisions of the army, which were ordered to hasten forward." Taylor wrote later that he returned to Lee under the impression that Ewell would attack.

Ewell found several reasons why such an attack was not practicable, while his subordinates urged action. Major General Edward Johnson's division was the last of Ewell's to reach Gettysburg. Major Henry Kyd Douglas of Johnson's staff arrived with news that Johnson was perhaps an hour away but could then be brought into action. Ewell allegedly remarked that he had brought his troops onto the field but did not have additional orders from Lee justifying an advance. (An odd position if the Taylor exchange already occurred.) Unfortunately for Ewell, many of those present and now closely observing him had previously served under Stonewall Jackson. Major Sandie Pendleton, Ewell's assistant adjutant general who had previously been supportive of his new boss, invoked the martyred Jackson, "Oh, for the presence and inspiration of Old Jack for just one hour!" Aide de Camp James Power Smith considered Ewell was "as true a Confederate soldier as ever went into battle, [but he] was simply waiting for orders, when every moment of the time could not be balanced with gold." In other words, Jackson's ex-staffers thought Ewell failed to take the initiative, as Jackson presumably would have, and let opportunity slip away at a critical moment.

Since the enthusiasm of Ewell's generals seemed conditional upon receiving support from A. P. Hill, Ewell sent Smith to Lee with a request for that assistance. Smith located Lee and was told, "Our people are not all up yet, and I have no troops with which to occupy this higher ground." Yet, Lee also declined to commit any portion of Richard Anderson's division of Hill's Third Corps which arrived that afternoon and moved into a reserve position. Thomas's brigade from Pender's division also remained in support of artillery and unutilized. According to Smith, however,

Lee told him to inform Ewell, "he regretted that his people were not up to support him on the right, but he wished him to take the Cemetery Hill if it were possible; and that he would ride over and see him very soon."

Ewell determined instead that Johnson's division would take Culp's Hill when they arrived on the field. "I could not bring artillery to bear on it, and all the troops with me were jaded by twelve hours' marching and fighting ... Cemetery Hill was not assailable from the town, and I determined, with Johnson's division, to take possession of a wooded hill to my left [Culp's Hill], on a line with and commanding Cemetery Hill." Would an assault on Cemetery Hill have succeeded? Opinions were divided, but the attack did not happen and "what-if" scenarios are

▲ Major General Edward Johnson led the last of Ewell's divisions to arrive on the battlefield. General Ewell intended for Johnson to occupy Culp's Hill, but time and Hancock's placement of troops there worked against the Confederates. (Library of Congress)

An Unavoidable Battle

Large Civil War armies did not move easily or quickly. Longstreet's desire to simply move Lee's army between Meade's army and Washington sounded good on paper and even better in hindsight, but Lee had several rational reasons for rejecting the proposal.

Despite the first day's successes, Lee's army was now concentrated about ten miles east of South Mountain, which had screened his northern movements and protected supply and communication lines back to Virginia. Continuing away from the mountains and deeper into the enemy's country, while in the presence of the enemy, would threaten those supplies and communications.

The continued absence of Stuart's cavalry meant they were unavailable to scout or screen such a risky maneuver. By the evening of July 1, Stuart was in Carlisle and most of his command finally reunited with the Army of Northern Virginia on the afternoon of July 2. Thanks partially to Stuart's absence, Lee had no means of determining how much of the Army of the Potomac was still on the march south of Gettysburg. An unscreened movement by Lee's entire army risked trapping the Confederates between multiple elements of enemy forces, rather than fighting Longstreet's carefully pre-planned battle.

It was likely that the Northerners would receive reinforcements while the Confederates would receive none. On the other hand, Chancellorsville had shown Lee that aggressive maneuver and fighting could overcome a numerically superior opponent. Lee understood these factors when he wrote, "A battle thus became, in a measure, unavoidable. Encouraged by the successful issue of the engagement of the first day, and in view of the valuable results that would ensue from the defeat of the army of General Meade, it was thought advisable to renew the attack."

unprovable. Yet, post-war history placed Ewell's indecision as one of the major factors in the battle's loss.

While Ewell and A. P. Hill combined for the day's victory, James Longstreet's First Corps spent most of the hours on the march. For much of July 1, the First Corps trudged east through South Mountain, Cashtown, and along Chambersburg Pike. They heard the low, distant rumblings of battle but were stuck behind the tail of Hill's column and then behind Johnson's supply wagons that entered the road ahead of them. General Longstreet decided to ride ahead of his command and locate General Lee, which he eventually did west of Gettysburg.

As the two men studied the situation with their field glasses, Longstreet was quite pleased by the developments. Longstreet maintained later that he told Lee:

> All we have to do is to throw our army around by their left, and we shall interpose between the Federal army and Washington. We can get a strong position and wait, and if they fail to attack us, we shall have everything in condition to move back tomorrow night in the direction of Washington, selecting beforehand a good position into which we can place our troops to receive battle next day.

Lee surprised Longstreet, however, when he responded decisively: "No, the enemy is there, and I am going to attack him there." Longstreet again reminded Lee of "our original plans," but Lee again rejected the proposal. Longstreet realized that Stuart's still-absent cavalry was causing much of Lee's anxiety, and he could see that Lee was in no mind to entertain further debate. The subordinate decided not to "push the matter but determined the renew the subject the next morning."

Richard Ewell's inability to capture Cemetery Hill is defensible. His failure to occupy Culp's Hill is less so. While General Hancock had placed portions of the First Corps on Culp's Hill, they were hardly in overwhelming force during these hours. Confederate General Isaac Trimble wrote afterwards that he made a reconnaissance of the position while Ewell supposedly paced indecisively. Trimble urged occupation of the hill with a brigade and artillery. According to Trimble, Ewell replied testily, "When I need advice from a junior officer, I generally ask it." General Early meanwhile urged, "If you do not go up there tonight, it will cost you ten thousand men to get up there tomorrow."

General Lee paid a visit to the Second Corps officers and discussed making the next day's attack along Ewell's front. The assembled generals, particularly Jubal Early, argued that the terrain did not favor the idea. Lee then proposed withdrawing Ewell's corps to the Confederate right, but this too was resisted. After this meeting, Lee sent a message to Ewell confirming his corps was to move to the right "in case it could not be used to advantage where it was." But Ewell and Lee were not finished with each other for the evening. Ewell met with Lee again and "represented to the commanding general that the hill above referred to [Culp's Hill] was unoccupied by the enemy … and that it commanded their position and made it untenable, so far as I could judge." Lee again allowed Ewell to remain in his position.

It was after midnight when Ewell finally ordered Edward Johnson to take possession of Culp's Hill. General Johnson replied, however, that he had already sent a reconnoitering party to the hill, but

▲ Modern view toward the north slope of Culp's Hill and the 7th Indiana monument. A night-time collision on these slopes between the Hoosiers and a reconnaissance party from Johnson's division prevented further July 1 attempts to capture the hill. (Author's photo)

▶ By the end of July 1, Hancock and Howard had established a formidable position on Cemetery Hill. Both armies would commit to fight again on the following day. Howard's equestrian statue is to the left of the photo, while Hancock's is to the right. (Author's photo)

they were fired upon as they approached the summit. Johnson's men had run into pickets from the 7th Indiana along the north slope. Believing they encountered "a superior force of the enemy" which captured two of their party, the remainder of Johnson's men withdrew. Ewell instructed Johnson to refrain from attacking the position until further confirmation was received of the enemy's occupation. "Day was now breaking," Ewell wrote, "and it was too late for any change of place." The Second Corps would attempt taking Culp's Hill later on July 2 and then again on July 3, but with much heavier losses as Jubal Early predicted. A campaign that started promisingly for Ewell at Second Winchester, and continued through the assaults of July 1, now regressed into his mistakenly persuading Lee that he could carry Culp's Hill.

Meanwhile, with Henry Slocum finally on the field to take command, and Dan Sickles's Third Corps also arriving from Emmitsburg, Hancock departed for a return to Taneytown at around 7:00 p.m. General Meade already issued orders for the remainder of the Army of the Potomac to concentrate at Gettysburg. The commanding general and several staffers departed Taneytown for Gettysburg shortly after 10:00 p.m. Any earlier thoughts of concentrating along Pipe Creek in Maryland were scuttled in favor of a battle in Pennsylvania.

Meade's party arrived on Cemetery Hill somewhere around 1:00 a.m. on July 2 and was met by a party of officers that included generals Howard, Slocum, Warren, and Sickles. Meade inquired, "Is this the place to fight the battle?" The assembled generals agreed on the defensibility of their position. Both Slocum and Howard expressed optimism that it could be held. "I am glad to hear you say so, gentlemen," Meade replied. "I have already ordered the other corps commanders to concentrate here, and it is too late to change."

Afterword

July 1, 1863, was one of the bloodiest single days of the American Civil War. A continued battle at Gettysburg was now unavoidable as both commanding generals Meade and Lee committed to bringing their remaining forces to Gettysburg.

Both armies fought at Gettysburg after having reorganized in the previous weeks. At every level, many officers were leading only their first or second major engagements. Some rose to the task while others were lacking. The ascension of Ewell and Hill to Army of Northern Virginia corps commands were probably the most notable reorganizational results. Lee's inability to personally manage both men in the battle's opening phases certainly wielded July 1 results that had direct consequences on the battle's outcome.

In the Army of the Potomac, George Meade inherited a recently defeated army that was ripe with political intrigue, exhibited dysfunction within some units, and had several new subordinate officers of their own. From Taneytown on July 1, Meade was unable to exert any personal battlefield leadership, but he did an excellent job putting the army in position to converge on Gettysburg, while also establishing supplies and logistical operations that do receive as much play in history books.

◄ Robert E. Lee headquartered himself at the Mary Thompson residence. Located along the Chambersburg Pike and at the foot of Seminary Ridge, Lee began planning his next moves. (Gettysburg National Military Park)

▲ This photograph of dead United States soldiers was taken sometime between July 4–7 and titled, "A Harvest of Death." The precise location of this image remains unknown, but some historians have proposed the first day's battlefield near McPherson Ridge as the site. (Library of Congress)

Was there a winner on July 1 at Gettysburg? Officers seldom reported casualties by day, making precise daily losses impossible to calculate. On the Union side, the First and Eleventh corps likely combined for about 9,000 total losses. That number exceeded 40% casualties in the First Corps and a slightly lower rate in the Eleventh. Some give credit to both corps for fighting and delaying the Confederate advances until Meade's army concentrated on Cemetery Hill. Both units were also essentially non-factors in the remaining battle, although subsequent events demonstrated that Meade had the strength and position to win the battle largely without them. Reynolds's loss was significant not only at the personal level,

but because of the ripple effect it had throughout the day's actions. His early departure led to numerous temporary elevations for Howard, Doubleday, Schurz, and others throughout both corps that impacted leadership and decision making.

For the Army of Northern Virginia, combined July 1 losses under Ewell and A. P. Hill were approximately 6,500. Unfortunately for Lee's smaller army, some commands that were mauled on July 1 would be called upon again before the battle concluded. Heth's division, for example, played a front-line role in the Pickett–Pettigrew–Trimble assault on July 3 at a greatly reduced strength.

Numbers do not tell the entire story. The confidence gained by these apparent military successes on July 1 encouraged Lee to renew the attack on subsequent days with less favorable results. In driving the Union forces from the fields west and north of Gettysburg, Lee's army unwittingly pushed the Army of the Potomac into a stronger position which caused the Northerners to win the battle on July 2–3.

A battle brought on by subordinate officers became unavoidable for both armies. The next day, July 2, would bring more fighting and bloodshed to Gettysburg.

Further Reading

Benjamin, Charles F. "Hooker's Appointment and Removal." In *Battles and Leaders of the Civil War*, edited by Robert U. Johnson and Clarence C. Buel, 3:239–43.

Brown, Kent Masterson. *Meade at Gettysburg: A Study in Command*. Chapel Hill, NC: University of North Carolina Press, 2021.

Busey, John W. and David G. Martin. *Regimental Strengths and Losses at Gettysburg*. Hightstown, NJ: Longstreet House, 1994.

Coddington, Edwin B. *The Gettysburg Campaign: A Study in Command*. Dayton, OH: Morningside Bookshop, 1979.

Dalton, Andrew. *Beyond the Run: The Emanuel Harmon Farm at Gettysburg*. Gettysburg, PA: Ten Roads Publishing, 2013.

Dawes, Rufus R. *Service with the Sixth Wisconsin Volunteers*. Marietta, OH: E.R. Alderman & Sons, 1890.

Doubleday, Abner. *Chancellorsville and Gettysburg*. Stamford, CT: Longmeadow Press, 1996. Reprint of the 1882 edition.

Floyd, Steven A. *Commanders and Casualties at the Battle of Gettysburg: The Comprehensive Order of Battle*. Gettysburg, PA: Gettysburg Publishing, 2014.

Frassanito, William A. *Early Photography at Gettysburg*. Gettysburg, PA: Thomas Publications, 1995.

Freeman, Douglas Southall. *Lee's Lieutenants*. New York: Charles Scribner's Sons, 1944.

Gallagher, Gary, editor. *The First Day at Gettysburg: Essays on Confederate and Union Leadership*. Kent, OH: Kent State University Press, 1992.

Gottfried, Bradley M. *Brigades of Gettysburg*. Cambridge, MA: Da Capo Press, 2002.

Hawthorne, Frederick. *Gettysburg: Stories of Men and Monuments*. Gettysburg, PA: Association of Licensed Battlefield Guides, 1988.

Hessler, James A. *Sickles at Gettysburg: The Controversial Civil War General Who Committed Murder, Abandoned Little Round Top, and Declared Himself the Hero of Gettysburg*. El Dorado Hills, CA: Savas Beatie, 2009.

Himmer, Robert. "A Matter of Time: The Issuance of the Pipe Creek Circular." *Gettysburg Magazine* 46 (July 2012): 7–18.

Hoke, Jacob. *The Great Invasion*. Gettysburg, PA: Stan Clark Military Books, 1992. Reprint of the 1887 edition.

Howard, Oliver O. "The Eleventh Corps at Chancellorsville." In *Battles and Leaders of the Civil War*, edited by Robert U. Johnson and Clarence C. Buel, 3:189–202.

Hunt, Henry J. "The First Day at Gettysburg." In *Battles and Leaders of the Civil War*, edited by Robert U. Johnson and Clarence C. Buel, 3:255–83.

Hyde, Bill, editor. *The Union Generals Speak: The Meade Hearings on the Battle of Gettysburg*. Baton Rouge, LA: Louisiana State University Press, 2003.

Ivanoff, Carolyn. *We Fought at Gettysburg: Firsthand Accounts by the Survivors of the 17th Connecticut Volunteer Infantry*. Gettysburg, PA: Gettysburg Publishing, 2023.

Laino, Philip. *Gettysburg Campaign Atlas*. Dayton, OH: Gatehouse Press, 2009.

Martin, David G. *Gettysburg July 1*. Cambridge, MA: Da Capo Press, 2003.

Nye, Wilbur Sturtevant. *Here Come the Rebels!* Dayton, OH: Morningside Bookshop, 1988.

Pfanz, Donald C. *Richard Ewell: A Soldier's Life*. Chapel Hill, NC: University of North Carolina Press, 1998.

Pfanz, Harry W. *Gettysburg: The First Day*. Chapel Hill, NC: The University of North Carolina Press, 2001.

Samito, Christian G., editor. *Fear Was Not in Him: The Civil War Letters of Major General Francis C. Barlow, U.S.A.* New York: Fordham University Press, 2004.

Sears, Stephen W. *Chancellorsville*. New York: Houghton Mifflin Company, 1996.

Smith, Timothy H. *John Burns: "The Hero of Gettysburg."* Gettysburg, PA: Thomas Publications, 2000.

Tagg, Larry. *The Generals of Gettysburg*. Cambridge, MA: Da Capo Press, 2003.

Trudeau, Noah Andre. *Gettysburg: A Testing of Courage*. New York: HarperCollins, 2002.

The War of the Rebellion: A Compilation of the Official Records of the Union and Confederate Armies. Washington, DC: Government Printing Office, 1880–1901.

Warner, Ezra J. *Generals in Blue: Lives of the Union Commanders*. Baton Rouge, LA: Louisiana State University Press, 2013. Reprint of the 1964 edition.

———. *Generals in Gray: Lives of the Confederate Commanders*. Baton Rouge, LA: Louisiana State University Press, 2013. Reprint of the 1959 edition.

Wittenberg, Eric J. *John Buford at Gettysburg: A History and Walking Tour*. El Dorado Hills, CA: Savas Beatie, 2014.

Wynstra, Robert J. *The Rashness of the Hour: Politics, Gettysburg, and the Downfall of Brigadier General Alfred Iverson*. El Dorado Hills, CA: Savas Beatie, 2010.

Index